THE *Essential*
EDWARD FITZGERALD

THE *Essential*
EDWARD FITZGERALD

RUBÁIYÁT OF OMAR KHAYYÁM
SALÁMÁN AND ABSÁL

TRANSLATED BY

Edward FitzGerald

COMPILED AND EDITED BY

Simon Prichard

CARRIGBOY CLASSICS

Published by
CARRIGBOY
Wells, Somerset, England.
www.carrigboy.co.uk
typecarrigboy@btinternet.com

© CARRIGBOY 2014

Print edition ISBN 978-1-910388-02-0
Kindle eBook ISBN 978-1-910388-01-3
ePub eBook ISBN 978-1-910388-00-6

A CIP catalogue record for this book is available from the British Library.

Cover design and print origination by CARRIGBOY.
Printed by CreateSpace.

CONTENTS

FOREWORD

Welcome to the CARRIGBOY CLASSICS SERIES, a specially chosen series of books drawn from the very best of the World's classical literature.

All of the CARRIGBOY CLASSICS SERIES are professionally re-typeset for quality, consistency and clarity of presentation. A CARRIGBOY CLASSIC title is simultaneously published in traditional print format as well as in the most popular eBook formats, all from the same, newly-set, original and unabridged source material.

CARRIGBOY have been designing and typesetting historical and academic works for over twenty years, and in the CARRIGBOY CLASSICS SERIES you can be assured of the highest professional standards, designed to ensure that the presentation does not obscure the content; that the format is immediately apparent, consistent and clear; and that the reading of a CARRIGBOY CLASSIC is always a taken-for-granted pleasure.

Simon Prichard
Well, 2014

INTRODUCTION

THE *Essential* EDWARD FITZGERALD

Here in one volume are the collected chief works of the Victorian writer and poet, Edward FitzGerald, complete with original notes, prefaces, glossary and appendix.

For the great majority of English readers, the Rubáiyát of Omar Khayyám means only these particular translations, the first, second and fifth editions done so divinely well by FitzGerald, when the Victorian Age of Empire was at its height.

Here also is his less well-known translation of the mystical Súfi allegory, Salámán and Absál, by the Persian scholar and poet, Jámí, as well as FitzGerald's biographies of both Omar Khayyám and Jámí.

OMAR KHAYYÁM

The Astronomer-Poet of Persia

Preface to the first edition, 1859

OMAR KHAYYÁM was born at Naishápúr in Khorassán in the latter half of our Eleventh, and died within the First Quarter of our Twelfth Century. The slender Story of his Life is curiously twined about that of two other very considerable Figures in their Time and Country: one of them, Hasan al Sabbáh, whose very Name has lengthen'd down to us as a terrible Synonym for Murder: and the other (who tells the Story of all Three) Nizám-ul-Mulk, Vizyr to Alp the Lion and Malik Shah, Son and Grandson of Toghrul Beg the Tartar, who had wrested Persia from the feeble Successor of Mahmúd the Great, and founded that Seljukian Dynasty which finally roused Europe into the Crusades. This Nizám-ul-Mulk, in his *Wasjat*—or *Testament*—which he wrote and left as a Memorial for future Statesmen—relates the following, as quoted in the *Calcutta Review*, No. 59, from Mirkhond's *History of the Assassins.*

'One of the greatest of the wise men of Khorassán was the Imám Mowaffak of Naishápúr, a man highly honoured and reverenced—may God rejoice his soul; his illustrious years exceeded eighty-five, and it was the universal belief that

3

every boy who read the Koran or studied the traditions in his presence would assuredly attain to honour and happiness. For this cause did my father send me from Tús to Naishápúr with Abd-u-samad, the doctor of law, that I might employ myself in study and learning under the guidance of that illustrious teacher. Towards me he ever turned an eye of favour and kindness, and as his pupil I felt for him extreme affection and devotion, so that I passed four years in his service. When I first came there, I found two other pupils of mine own age newly arrived, Hakim Omar Khayyám, and the ill-fated Ben Sabbáh. Both were endowed with sharpness of wit and the highest natural powers; and we three formed a close friendship together. When the Imám rose from his lectures they used to join me, and we repeated to each other the lessons we had heard. Now Omar was an native of Naishápúr, while Hasan Ben Sabbáh's father was one Ali, a man of austere life and practice, but heretical in his creed and doctrine. One day Hasan said to me and to Khayyám,

"It is a universal belief that the pupils of the Imám Mowaffak will attain to fortune. Now, even if we *all* do not attain thereto, without doubt one of us will; what then shall be our mutual pledge and bond?"

We answered, "Be it what you please."

"Well" he said, "let us make a vow, that to whomsoever this fortune falls, he shall share it equally with the rest, and reserve no pre-eminence for himself."

"Be it so," we both replied, and on these terms we mutually pledged our words.

Years rolled on, and I went from Khorassán to Transoxima, and wandered to Ghazni and Cabul; and when I returned, I was invested with office, and rose to be administrator of affairs during the Sultanate of Sultan Alp Arslán.'

He goes on to state, that years passed by, and both his old school-friends found him out and came and claimed a share in his good fortune, according to his school-day vow. The Vizier was generous and kept his word. Hasan demanded a place in the government, which the Sultan granted at the Vizier's request; but discontented with a gradual rise, he plunged into the maze of intrigue of an oriental court, and, failing in a base attempt to supplant his benefactor, he was disgraced and fell. After many mishaps and wanderings, Hasan became the head of the Persian sect of the *Ismailians*—a party of fanatics who had long murmured in obscurity, but rose to an evil eminence under the guidance of his strong and evil will. In A.D. 1090, he seized the castle of Alamut, in the province of Rúdbar, which lies in the mountainous tract south of the Caspian Sea; and it was from this mountain home he obtained that evil celebrity among the Crusaders as THE OLD MAN OF THE MOUNTAINS, and spread terror through the Mohammedan world; and it is yet disputed whether the word *Assassin* which they have left in the language of modern Europe as their dark memorial, is derived from the *hashish*, or opiate of hemp-leaves (the Indian *bhang*), with which they maddened themselves to the sullen pitch of oriental desperation, or from the name of the founder of the dynasty, whom we have seen in his quiet collegiate days, at Naishápúr. One of the countless victims of the Assassin's dagger was Nizám-ul-Mulk himself, the old school-boy friend.

Omar Khayyám also came to the Vizier to claim his share; but not to ask for title or office.

'The greatest boon you can confer on me ...'

he said,

'... is to let me live in a corner under the shadow of your fortune, to spread wide the advantages of Science, and pray for your long life and prosperity.'

The Vizier tells us, that, when he found Omar was really sincere in his refusal, he pressed him no further, but granted him a yearly pension of 1200 *mikháls* of gold, from the treasury of Naishápúr.

At Naishápúr thus lived and died Omar Khayyám, 'busied,' adds the Vizier,

> 'in winning knowledge of every kind, and especially in Astronomy, wherein he attained to a very high pre-eminence. Under the Sultanate of Malik Shah, he came to Merv, and obtained great praise for his proficiency in science, and the Sultan showered favours upon him.'

When Malik Shah determined to reform the calendar, Omar was one of the eight learned men employed to do it; the result was the *Jaláli* era (so called from *Jalál-ud-din,* one of the king's names);

> 'a computation of time, ...'

says Gibbon,

> '... which surpasses the Julian, and approaches the accuracy of the Gregorian style.'

He is also the author of some astronomical tables, entitled *Zíji-Malik-sháhí,* and the French have lately republished and translated an Arabic Treatise of his on Algebra.

These severer Studies, and his Verses, which, though happily fewer than any Persian Poet's, and, though perhaps fugitively composed, the Result of no fugitive Emotion or Thought, are probably the Work and Event of his Life, leaving little else to record. Perhaps he liked a little Farming too, so often as he speaks of the "Edge of the Tilth" on which he loved to rest with his *Diwán* of Verse, his Loaf—and his Wine.

His *Takhallus* or poetical name (Khayyám) signifies a Tent-maker, and he is said to have at one time exercised that trade, perhaps before Nizám-ul-Mulk's generosity raised him to independence. Many Persian poets similarly derive their names from their occupations; thus we have Attár, a druggist, Assar, an oil presser, etc. (Though all these, like our Smiths, Archers, Millers, Fletchers, etc., may simply retain the Surname of an hereditary calling). Omar himself alludes to his name in the following whimsical lines:

KHAYYÁM, who stitched the tents of science,
Has fallen in grief's furnace and been suddenly
    burned;
The shears of Fate have cut the tent ropes of
    his life,
And the broker of Hope has sold him for
    nothing!

We have only one more anecdote to give of his Life, and that relates to the close; related in the anonymous preface which is sometimes prefixed to his poems; it has been printed in the Persian in the appendix to Hyde's *Veterum Persarum Religio*, p. 499; and D'Herbelot alludes to it in his *Bibliothèque*, under *Khiam*.[1]

'It is written in the chronicles of the ancients that this King of the Wise, Omar Khayyám, died at Naishápúr in the year of the Hegira 517 (AD1123); in science he was unrivalled—the very paragon of his age. Khwájah Nizámi of Samarcand who was one of his pupils, relates the following story:

"I often used to hold conversations with my teacher, Omar Khayyám, in a garden; and one day he said to me,

'my tomb shall be in a spot, where the north wind may scatter roses over it.'

I wondered at the words he spake, but I knew that his were no idle words. Years after, when I chanced to revisit Naishápúr, I went to his final resting place, and lo! it was just outside a garden, and trees laden with fruit stretched their boughs over the garden wall, and dropped their flowers

---

1 Though *he* attributes the story to a Khiam, "*Philosophe Musulman qui a vécu en Odeur de Sainteté dans la Fin du premier et le Commencement du second Siécle*", no part of which, exccpt the "*Philosophe*", can apply to *our* Khayyám, who, however, may claim the Story as *his*, on the Score of Rubáiyát 77 and 78 of the present Version. The Rashness of the Words, according to D'Herbelot, consisted in being so opposed to those in the Korán: " No man knows where he shall die."

upon his tomb, so as the stone was hidden under them.'"

Thus far—without fear of Trespass—from the *Calcutta Review*.

Though the Sultan "shower'd Favours upon him" Omar's Epicurean Audacity of Thought and Speech caused him to be regarded askance in his own Time and Country. He is said to have been especially hated and dreaded by the Súfis, whose Practice he ridiculed, and whose Faith amounts to little more than his own when stript of the Mysticism and formal Compliment to Islamism which Omar would not hide under. Their Poets, including Háfiz, who are (with the exception of Firdúsi) the most considerable in Persia, borrowed largely, indeed, of Omar's material, but turning it to a mystical Use more convenient to Themselves and the People they address'd; a People quite as quick of Doubt as of Belief; quite as keen of the Bodily Senses as of the Intellectual; and delighting in a cloudy Element compounded of all, in which they could float luxuriously between Heaven and Earth, and this World and the Next, on the wings of a poetical expression, that could be recited indifferently whether at the Mosque or the Tavern. Omar was too honest of Heart as well as of Head for this. Having failed (however mistakenly) of finding any Providence but Destiny, and any World but This, he set about making the most of it; preferring rather to soothe the Soul through the Senses into Acquiescence with Things as they were, than to perplex it with vain mortifications after what they *might be*. It has been seen that his Worldly Desires, however, were not exorbitant; and he very likely takes a humorous pleasure in exaggerating them above that Intellect in whose exercise he must have found great pleasure, though not in a Theological direction. However this may be, his Worldly Pleasures are what they profess to be without any Pretence at divine Allegory: his Wine is the veritable Juice of the Grape: his Tavern, where it was to be had: his Sáki, the Flesh and Blood that poured it out for him: all which, and where the Roses were in Bloom, was all he profess'd to want of this World or to expect of Paradise.

The Mathematic Faculty, too, which regulated his Fancy, and condensed his Verse to a Quality and Quantity unknown in Persian, perhaps in Oriental, Poetry, help'd by its very virtue perhaps to render him less popular with his countrymen. If the Greeks were Children in Gossip, what does Persian Literature imply but a *Second Childishness* of Garrulity? And certainly if no *ungeometric* Greek was to enter Plato's School of Philosophy, no so unchastised a Persian should enter on the Race of Persian Verse, with its "fatal Facility" of running on long after Thought is winded! But

Omar was not only the single Mathematician of his Country's Poets; he was also of that older Time and stouter Temper, before the native Soul of Persia was quite broke by a foreign Creed as well as foreign Conquest. Like his great Predecessor Firdúsi, who was as little of a *Mystic*; who scorned to use even a *Word* of the very language in which the New Faith came clothed; and who was suspected, not of Omar's Irreligion indeed, but of secretly clinging to the ancient Fire-Religion of Zerdusht, of which so many of the Kings he sang were Worshippers.

For whatever Reason, however, Omar, as before said, has never been popular in his own Country, and therefore has been but charily transmitted abroad. The MSS of his poems, mutilated beyond the average Casualties of Oriental Transcription, are so rare in the East as scarce to have reacht Westward at all, in spite of all that Arms and Science have brought us. There is none at the India House, none at the Bibliothèque Impériale of Paris. We know but of one in England; No. 140 of the Ouseley MSS at the Bodleian, written at Shiraz, AD 1460. This contains but 158 Rubáiyát. One in the Asiatic Society's Library of Calcutta (of which we have a Copy) contains (and yet incomplete) 516, though swelled to that by all kinds of Repetition and Corruption. So Von Hammer speaks of *his* Copy as containing about 200, while Dr. Sprenger catalogues the Lucknow MS at double that Number.

The Scribes, too, of the Oxford and Calcutta MSS seem to do their Work under a sort of Protest; each beginning with a Tetrastich (whether genuine or not) taken out of its alphabetical order; the Oxford with one of Apology; the Calcutta with one of Execration too stupid for Omar's' even had Omar been stupid enough to execrate himself[2]

The Reviewer, who translates the foregoing Particulars of Omar's Life, and some of his Verse into Prose, concludes by comparing him with Lucretius, both in natural Temper and Genius, and as acted upon by the Circumstances in which he lived. Both indeed men of subtle Intellect and high Imagination, instructed in Learning beyond their day, and of Hearts passionate for Truth and Justice; who justly revolted from their Country's false Religion, and false, or foolish, Devotion to it; but who yet fell short of replacing what they subverted by any such better *Hope* as others, upon whom no better *Faith* had dawned, had yet made a Law to themselves. Lucretius, indeed, with such material as Epicurus furnished, consoled himself with the construction of a Machine that needed no Constructor, and acting by a Law that implied no Lawgiver; and so composing himself into a Stoical rather than Epicurean severity of Attitude, sat

---

2 "Since this Paper was written" (adds the Reviewer in a note), "we have met with a copy of a very rare Edition, printed at Calcutta in 1836. This contains 438 Tetrastichs, with an Appendix containing 54 others not found in some MSS."

down to contemplate the mechanical Drama of the Universe of which he was part Actor; himself and all about him (as in his own sublime Description of the Roman Theatre), coloured with the lurid reflex of the Curtain that was suspended between them and the outer Sun. Omar, more desperate, or more careless, of any such laborious System as resulted in nothing more than hopeless Necessity, flung his own Genius and Learning with a bitter jest into the general Ruin which their insufficient glimpses only served to reveal; and, yielding his Senses to the actual Rose and Vine, only *diverted* his thoughts by balancing ideal possibilities of Fate, Freewill, Existence and Annihilation; with an oscillation that so generally inclined to the negative and lower side, as to make such Stanzas as the following exceptions to his general Philosophy—

Oh, if my Soul can fling his Dust aside, and
　　naked on the Air of Heaven ride,
Is't not a Shame, is't not a Shame for Him so
　　long in this Clay Suburb to abide!

Or is *that* but a Tent, where rests anon a
　　Sultán to his Kingdom Passing on,
And which the swarthy Chamberlain shall
　　strike then when the Sultán rises to be
　　gone?

With regard to the present Translation. The original Rubáiyát (as, missing an Arabic Guttural, these *Tetrastichs* are more musically called), are independent Stanzas, consisting each of four Lines of equal, though varied, Prosody, sometimes *all* rhyming, but oftener (as here attempted) the third line suspending the Cadence—by which the last atones with the former Two. Something as in the Greek Alcaic, where the third line seems to lift and suspend the Wave that falls over in the last. As usual with such kind of Oriental Verse, the Rubáiyát follow one another according to Alphabetic Rhymes—a strange Farrago of Grave and Gay. Those here selected are strung into something of an Eclogue, with perhaps a less than equal proportion of the "Drink and make-merry," which (genuine or not) recurs over-frequently in the Original. For Lucretian as Omar's Genius might be, he cross'd that darker Mood with much of Olivier de Basselin Humour. Anyway, the Result is sad enough: saddest perhaps when most ostentatiously merry: anyway, fitter to move Sorrow than Anger toward the old Tentmaker, who, after vainly endeavouring to unshackle his Steps from Destiny, and to catch some authentic Glimpse of To-morrow, fell back upon To-day (which has out-lasted so many To-morrows!) as the only Ground he got to stand upon, however, momentarily slipping from under his Feet.

RUBÁIYÁT

of

OMAR KHAYYÁM

FIRST EDITION, 1859

I

AWAKE! for Morning in the Bowl
of Night
Has flung the Stone that puts the
Stars to Flight:
And Lo! the Hunter of the East has
caught
The Sultán's Turret in a Noose of
Light.

II

DREAMING when Dawn's Left
Hand was in the Sky
I heard a Voice within the Tavern cry
"Awake, my Little ones, and fill the
Cup
Before Life's Liquor in its Cup be
dry."

III

AND, as the Cock crew, those who stood before
The Tavern shouted—"Open then the
    Door!
You know how little while we have
    to stay,
And, once departed, may return no
    more."

IV

NOW the New Year reviving old Desires,
The thoughtful Soul to Solitude
    retires,
Where the WHITE HAND of MOSES
    on the Bough
Puts out, and Jesus from the Ground
    suspires.

V

IRAM indeed is gone with all its
  Rose,
And Jamshýd's Sev'n-ring'd Cup
  where no one knows;
But still the Vine her ancient ruby
  yields,
And still a Garden by the Water
  blows.

VI

AND David's Lips are lock't; but
  in divine
High piping Pehleví, with "Wine!
  Wine! Wine!
Red Wine"—the Nightingale cries to
  the Rose
That yellow Cheek of hers to
  incarnadine.

VII

COME, fill the Cup, and in the
Fire of Spring
The Winter Garment of Repentance
    fling:
The Bird of Time has but a little way
To fly—and Lo ! the Bird is on the
    Wing.

VIII

AND look—a thousand Blossoms
with the Day
Woke—and a thousand scatter'd into
    Clay:
And this first Summer Month that
    brings the Rose
Shall take Jamshýd and Kaikobád
    away.

IX

BUT come with old Khayyám, and leave the Lot
Of Kaikobád and Kaikhosrú
    forgot:
Let Rustum lay about him as he will,
Or Hátim Tai cry Supper—heed them
    not.

X

WITH me along some Strip of
    Herbage strown
That just divides the desert from the
    sown,
Where name of Slave and Sultán
    scarce is known,
And pity Sultán Máhmúd on his
    Throne.

XI

HERE with a Loaf of Bread beneath the Bough,
A Flask of Wine, a Book of Verse and
    Thou
Beside me singing in the Wilderness—
And Wilderness is Paradise enow.

XII

"HOW sweet is mortal Sovranty!" —think some:
Others—"How blest the Paradise to
    come!"
Ah, take the Cash in hand and waive
    the Rest;
Oh, the brave Music of a distant
    Drum!

XIII

L OOK to the Rose that blows about us—"Lo,
Laughing," she says, "into the World I blow:
At once the silken Tassel of my Purse
Tear, and its Treasure on the Garden throw."

XIV

T HE Worldly Hope men set their Hearts upon
Turns Ashes—or it prospers; and anon,
Like Snow upon the Desert's dusty Face
Lighting a little Hour or two—is gone.

XV

AND those who husbanded the Golden Grain,
And those who flung it to the Winds like Rain,
Alike to no such aureate Earth are turn'd
As, buried once, Men want dug up again.

XVI

THINK, in this batter'd Caravanserai
Whose Doorways are alternate Night and Day,
How Sultán after Sultán with his Pomp
Abode his Hour or two, and went his way.

XVII

THEY say the Lion and the Lizard keep
The Courts where Jamshýd gloried
    and drank deep;
And Bahrám, that great Hunter—the
    Wild Ass
Stamps o'er his Head, and he lies fast
    asleep.

XVIII

I SOMETIMES think that never
    blows so red
The Rose as where some buried
    Cæsar bled;
That every Hyacinth the Garden
    wears
Dropt in its Lap from some once
    lovely Head.

XIX

AND this delightful Herb whose tender *Green*
Fledges the River's Lip on which we
    lean—
Ah, lean upon it lightly! for who
    knows
From what once lovely Lip it springs
    unseen!

XX

AH, my Belovéd, fill the Cup that
    clears
TO-DAY of past Regrets and future
    Fears—
TO-MORROW?—Why To-morrow I
    may be
Myself with Yesterday's Sev'n
    Thousand Years.

XXI

L O! some we loved, the loveliest
and best
That Time and Fate of all their
   Vintage prest,
Have drunk their Cup a Round or
   two before,
And one by one crept silently to
   Rest.

XXII

A ND we, who now make merry in
the Room
They left, and Summer dresses in her
   new Bloom,
Ourselves must we beneath the
   Couch of Earth
Descend, ourselves to make a
   Couch—for whom?

XXIII

AH, make the most of what we yet may spend.
Before we too into the Dust descend;
Dust into Dust, and under Dust, to
    lie,
Sans wine, sans Song, sans Singer, and
    sans End!

XXIV

ALIKE for those who for To-day Prepare,
And those that after a To-morrow
    stare,
A Muezzin from the Tower of
    Darkness cries
Fools! your Reward is neither Here
    nor There

XXV

WHY, all the Saints and Sages who discuss'd
Of the Two Worlds so learnedly, are
thrust
Like foolish Prophets forth; their
Words to Scorn
Are scatter'd, and their Mouths are
stopt with Dust.

XXVI

OH, come with old Khayyám, and
leave the Wise
To talk; one thing is certain, that Life
flies;
One thing is certain, and the Rest is
Lies;
The Flower that once has blown for
ever dies.

XXVII

MYSELF when young did eagerly frequent
Doctor and Saint, and heard great
  Argument
About it and about: but evermore
Came out by the same Door as in I
  went.

XXVIII

WITH them the Seed of Wisdom
  did I sow,
And with my own hand labour'd it to
  grow:
And this was all the Harvest that I
  reap'd—
"I came like Water, and like Wind I
  go."

XXIX

INTO this Universe, and *why* not knowing,
Nor *whence*, like Water willy-nilly flowing:
And out of it, as Wind along the Waste,
I know not *whither*, willy-nilly blowing.

XXX

WHAT, without asking, hither hurried *whence*?
And, without asking, *whither* hurried hence!
Another and another Cup to drown
The Memory of this Impertinence!

XXXI

UP from Earth's Centre through
the Seventh Gate
I rose, and on the Throne of Saturn
sate,
And many Knots unravel'd by the
Road;
But not the Knot of Human Death
and Fate.

XXXII

THERE was a Door to which I
found no Key:
There was a Veil past which I could
not see:
Some little Talk awhile of ME and
THEE
There seem'd—and then no more of
THEE and ME.

XXXIII

THEN to the rolling Heav'n itself I
   cried,
Asking, "What Lamp had Destiny to
   guide
Her little Children stumbling in the
   Dark?"
And—"A blind Understanding!"
   Heav'n replied.

XXXIV

THEN to this earthen Bowl did I
   adjourn
My Lip the secret Well of Life to
   learn:
And Lip to Lip it murmur'd—"While
   you live
Drink!—for once dead you never
   shall return."

XXXV

I THINK the Vessel, that with fugitive
Articulation answer'd, once did live,
And merry-make; and the cold Lip I
  kiss'd
How many Kisses might it take—and
  give!

XXXVI

FOR in the Market-place, one Dusk
  of Day,
I watch'd the Potter thumping his wet
  Clay:
And with its all obliterated Tongue
It murmur'd—"Gently Brother,
  gently, pray!"

XXXVII

AH, fill the Cup: what boots it to
repeat
How Time is slipping underneath our
Feet:
Unborn TO-MORROW, and dead
YESTERDAY,
Why fret about them if TO-DAY be
sweet!

XXXVIII

ONE moment in Annihilation's
Waste,
One Moment, of the Well of Life to
taste—
The Stars are setting and the Caravan
Starts for the Dawn of Nothing—Oh,
make haste!

XXXIX

HOW long, how long, in infinite Pursuit
Of This and That endeavour and
    dispute?
Better be merry with the fruitful
    Grape
Than sadden after none, or bitter,
    Fuit.

XL

YOU know, my Friends, how long
    since in my house
For a new Marriage I did make
    Carouse:
Divorced old barren Reason from my
    Bed,
And took the Daughter of the Vine to
    Spouse.

XLI

FOR "Is" and "Is-Not" though *with* Rule and Line,
And "Up-and-Down" *without*, I
  could define,
I yet in all I only cared to know,
Was never deep in anything but—
  Wine.

XLII

AND lately, by the Tavern Door agape,
Came stealing through the Dusk an
  Angel Shape
Bearing a Vessel on his shoulder; and
He bid me taste of it; and 'twas—the
  Grape!

XLIII

THE Grape that can with Logic
absolute
The Two-and-Seventy jarring Sects
confute:
The subtle Alchemist that in a Trice
Life's leaden Metal into Gold
transmute.

XLIV

THE mighty Máhmúd, the
victorious Lord,
That all the misbelieving and black
Horde
Of Fears and Sorrows that infest the
Soul
Scatters and slays with his enchanted
Sword.

XLV

BUT leave the Wise to wrangle, and with me
The Quarrel of the Universe let be:
And, in some corner of the Hubbub
    coucht,
Make Game of that which makes as
    much of Thee.

XLVI

FOR in and out, above, about,
    below,
'Tis nothing but a Magic Shadow-
    show,
Play'd in a Box whose Candle is the
    Sun,
Round which we phantom Figures
    come and go.

XLVII

AND if the Wine you drink, the Lip you Press,
End in the Nothing all Things end
    in—Yes—
Then fancy while Thou art, T'hou art
    but what
Thou shalt be—Nothing—Thou shalt
    not be less.

XLVIII

WHILE the Rose blows along the
    River Brink,
With old Khayyám the Ruby Vintage
    drink:
And when the Angel with the darker
    Draught
Draws up to Thee—take that, and do
    not shrink.

IL

'TIS all a Chequer-board of
    Nights and Days
Where Destiny with Men for Pieces
    plays:
Hither and thither moves, and mates,
    and slays.
And one by one back in the Closet
    lays.

L

THE Ball no Question makes of
    Ayes and Noes,
But Right or Left as strikes the Player
    goes;
And He that toss'd Thee down into
    the Field,
He knows about it all—HE knows—
    HE knows!

LI

THE Moving Finger writes; and,
        having writ,
Moves on; nor all thy Piety nor Wit
Shall lure it back to cancel half a
        Line,
Nor all thy Tears wash out a Word of
        it.

LII

AND that inverted Bowl we call
        The Sky,
Whereunder crawling coopt we live
        and die,
Lift not thy hands to *It* for help—for
        It
Rolls impotently on as Thou or I.

LIII

WITH Earth's first Clay They did
   the Last Man's knead,
And then of the Last Harvest sow'd
   the Seed:
Yea, the first Morning of Creation
   wrote
What the Last Dawn of Reckoning
   shall read.

LIV

I TELL Thee this—When, starting
   from the Goal,
Over the shoulders of the flaming
   Foal
Of Heav'n Parwín and Mushtara they
   flung,
In my predestin'd Plot of Dust and
   Soul.

LV

THE Vine had struck a Fibre; which about
If clings my Being—let the Súfi flout;
Of my Base Metal may be filed a Key,
That shall unlock the Door he howls
  without.

LVI

AND this I know; whether the one
  True Light,
Kindle to Love, or Wrath—consume
  me quite,
One glimpse of It within the Tavern
  caught
Better than in the Temple lost
  outright.

LVII

OH Thou, who didst with Pitfall
and with Gin
Beset the Road I was to wander in,
Thou wilt not with Predestination
  round
Enmesh me, and impute my Fall to
  Sin?

LVIII

OH, Thou, who Man of baser
Earth didst make,
And who with Eden didst devise the
  Snake;
For all the Sin wherewith the Face of
  Man
Is blacken'd, Man's Forgiveness
  give—and take!

Kúza-Náma

LIX

LISTEN again. One evening at the close
Of Ramazán, ere the better Moon
    arose,
In that old Potter's Shop I stood alone
With the clay Population round in
    Rows

LX

AND, strange to tell, among the
    Earthen Lot
Some could articulate, while others
    not:
And suddenly one more impatient
    cried—
"Who is the Potter, pray, and who the
    Pot?"

LXI

THEN said another—"Surely not in vain
My Substance from the common
    Earth was ta'en,
That He who subtly wrought me into
    Shape
Should stamp me back to common
    Earth again."

LXII

ANOTHER said—"Why, ne'er a peevish Boy
Would break the Bowl from which he
    drank in Joy;
Shall He that *made* the Vessel in pure
    Love
And Fancy, in an after Rage destroy!"

LXIII

NONE answer'd this; but after Silence spake
A Vessel of a more ungainly Make:
"They sneer at me for leaning all
    awry;
What! did the Hand then of the
    Potter shake!"

LXIV

SAID one— "Folks of a surly
    Tapster tell,
And daub his Visage with the Smoke
    of Hell;
They talk of some strict Testing of
    us—Pish!
He's a Good Fellow, and 'twill all be
    well."

LX

THEN said another with a long-
drawn Sigh,
"My Clay with long oblivion is gone
dry:
But, fill me with the old familiar
Juice,
Methinks I might recover by-and-bye!"

LXVI

SO while the Vessels one by one
were speaking,
One spied the little Crescent all were
seeking:
And then they jogg'd each other,
"Brother! Brother!
Hark to the Porter's Shoulder-knot
a-creaking!"

LXVII

AH, with the Grape my fading Life
provide,
And wash my Body whence the Life
has died,
And in a Windingsheet of vine-leaf
wrapt,
So bury me by some sweet Garden-
side.

LXVIII

THAT ev'n my buried Ashes such
a Snare
Of Perfume shall fling up into the Air,
As not a True Believer passing by
But shall be overtaken unaware.

LXIX

INDEED the Idols I have loved so
    long
Have done my Credit in Men's Eye
    much wrong:
Have drown'd my Honour in a
    shallow cup,
And sold my Reputation for a Song.

LXX

INDEED, indeed, Repentance oft
    before
I swore—but was I sober when I
    swore?
And then and then came Spring, and
    Rose-in-hand
My thread-bare Penitence apieces
    tore.

LXXI

AND much as Wine has play'd the Infidel,
And robb'd me of my Robe of
   Honour—well,
I often wonder what the Vintners buy
One half so precious as the Goods
   they sell.

LXXII

ALAS, that Spring should vanish with the Rose!
That Youth's sweet-scented
   Manuscript should close!
The Nightingale that in the Branches
   sang
Ah, whence, and whither flown again,
   who knows!

LXXIII

AH Love! could thou and I with
Fate conspire
To grasp this sorry Scheme of Things
entire,
Would not we shatter it to bits—and
then
Re-mould it nearer to the Heart's
Desire!

LXXIV

AH, Moon of my Delight who
know'st no wane,
The Moon of Heav'n is rising once
again:
How oft hereafter rising shall she
look
Through this same Garden after me—
in vain!

LXXV

AND when Thyself with shining Foot shall pass
Among the Guests Star-scatter'd on
  the Grass,
And in thy joyous Errand reach the
  Spot
Where I made one—turn down an
  empty Glass!

TÁMÁM SHUD.

Preface to the second edition, 1868

OMAR KHAYYÁM was born at Naishápúr in Khorassán in the latter half of our Eleventh, and died within the First Quarter of our Twelfth Century. The slender Story of his Life is curiously twined about that of two other very considerable Figures in their Time and Country: one of them, Hasan al Sabbáh, whose very Name has lengthen'd down to us as a terrible Synonym for Murder: and the other (who tells the Story of all Three) Nizám-ul-Mulk, Vizyr to Alp the Lion and Malik Shah, Son and Grandson of Toghrul Beg the Tartar, who had wrested Persia from the feeble Successor of Mahmúd the Great, and founded that Seljukian Dynasty which finally roused Europe into the Crusades. This Nizám-ul-Mulk, in his *Wasjat*—or *Testament*—which he wrote and left as a Memorial for future Statesmen—relates the following, as quoted in the *Calcutta Review*, No. 59, from Mirkhond's *History of the Assassins.*

'One of the greatest of the wise men of Khorassán was the Imám Mowaffak of Naishápúr, a man highly honoured and reverenced—may God rejoice his soul; his illustrious years exceeded eighty-five, and it was the universal belief that every boy who read the Koran or studied the traditions in his presence would assuredly attain to honour and happiness. For this cause did my father send me from Tús to Naishápúr with Abd-u-samad, the doctor of law, that I might employ myself in study and learning under the guidance of that illustrious teacher. Towards me he ever turned an eye of favour and kindness, and as his pupil I felt for him extreme affection and devotion, so that I passed four years in his service. When I first came there, I found two other pupils of mine own age newly arrived, Hakim Omar Khayyám, and the ill-fated Ben Sabbáh. Both were endowed with sharpness of wit and the highest natural powers; and we three formed a close friendship together. When the Imam rose from his lectures they used to join me, and we repeated to each other the lessons we had heard. Now Omar was an native of Naishápúr, while Hasan Ben Sabbáh's father was one Ali, a man of austere life and practice, but heretical in his creed and doctrine. One day Hasan said to me and to Khayyám,

"It is a universal belief that the pupils of the Imám Mowaffak will attain to fortune. Now, even if we *all* do not attain thereto, without doubt one of us will; what then shall be our mutual pledge and bond?"

We answered, "Be it what you please."

"Well" he said, "let us make a vow, that to whomsoever this fortune falls, he shall share it equally with the rest, and reserve no pre-eminence for himself."

"Be it so," we both replied, and on these terms we mutually pledged our words.

Years rolled on, and I went from Khorassán to Transoxima, and wandered to Ghazni and Cabul; and when I returned, I was invested with office, and rose to be administrator of affairs during the Sultanate of Sultan Alp Arslán.'

He goes on to state, that years passed by, and both his old school-friends found him out and came and claimed a share in his good fortune, according to his school-day vow. The Vizier was generous and kept his word. Hasan demanded a place in the government, which the Sultan granted at the Vizier's request; but discontented with a gradual rise, he plunged into the maze of intrigue of an oriental court, and, failing in a base attempt to supplant his benefactor, he was disgraced and fell. After many mishaps and wanderings, Hasan became the head of the Persian sect of the *Ismailians*—a party of fanatics who had long murmured in obscurity, but rose to an evil eminence under the guidance of his strong and evil will. In AD 1090, he seized the castle of Alamut, in the province of Rúdbar, which lies in the mountainous tract south of the Caspian Sea; and it was from this mountain home he obtained that evil celebrity among the Crusaders as THE OLD MAN OF THE MOUNTAINS, and spread terror through the Mohammedan world; and it is yet disputed whether the word *Assassin* which they have left in the language of modern Europe as their dark memorial, is derived from the *hashish*, or opiate of hemp-leaves (the Indian *bhang*), with which they maddened themselves to the sullen pitch of oriental desperation, or from the name of the founder of the dynasty, whom we have seen in his quiet collegiate days, at Naishápúr. One of the countless victims of the Assassin's dagger was Nizám-ul-Mulk himself, the old school-boy friend.

Omar Khayyám also came to the Vizier to claim his share; but not to ask for title or office.

'The greatest boon you can confer on me ...'

he said,

'... is to let me live in a corner under the shadow of your fortune, to spread wide the advantages of Science, and pray for your long life and prosperity.'

The Vizier tells us, that, when he found Omar was really sincere in his refusal, he pressed him no further, but granted him a yearly pension of 1200 *mikháls* of gold, from the treasury of Naishápúr.

At Naishápúr thus lived and died Omar Khayyám, 'busied,' adds the Vizier,

> 'in winning knowledge of every kind, and especially in Astronomy, wherein he attained to a very high pre-eminence. Under the Sultanate of Malik Shah, he came to Merv, and obtained great praise for his proficiency in science, and the Sultan showered favours upon him.'

When Malik Shah determined to reform the calendar, Omar was one of the eight learned men employed to do it; the result was the *Jaláli* era (so called from *Jalál-ud-din,* one of the king's names);

> 'a computation of time, ...'

says Gibbon,

> '... which surpasses the Julian, and approaches the accuracy of the Gregorian style.'

He is also the author of some astronomical tables, entitled *Zíji-Malik-sháhí*, and the French have lately republished and translated an Arabic Treatise of his on Algebra.

These severer Studies, and his Verses, which, though happily fewer than any Persian Poet's, and, though perhaps fugitively composed, the Result of no fugitive Emotion or Thought, are probably the Work and Event of his Life, leaving little else to record. Perhaps he liked a little Farming too, so often as he speaks of the "Edge of the Tilth" on which he loved to rest with his *Diwán* of Verse, his Loaf—and his Wine.

His *Takhallus* or poetical name (Khayyám) signifies a Tent-maker, and he is said to have at one time exercised that trade, perhaps before Nizám-ul-Mulk's generosity raised him to independence. Many Persian poets similarly derive their names from their occupations; thus we have Attár, a druggist, Assar, an oil presser, etc.[1] may simply retain the Surname of an hereditary calling). Omar himself alludes to his name in the following whimsical lines:

KHAYYÁM, who stitched the tents of science,
Has fallen in grief's furnace and been suddenly
burned;
The shears of Fate have cut the tent ropes of
his life,
And the broker of Hope has sold him for
nothing!

We have only one more anecdote to give of his Life, and that relates to the close; related in the

---

1 Though all these, like our Smiths, Archers, Millers, Fletchers, etc., may simply retain the Surname of an hereditary calling.

anonymous preface which is sometimes prefixed to his poems; it has been printed in the Persian in the appendix to Hyde's *Veterum Persarum Religio*, p. 499; and D'Herbelot alludes to it in his Bibliothèque, under *Khiam*.[2]

'It is written in the chronicles of the ancients that this King of the Wise, Omar Khayyám, died at Naishápúr in the year of the Hegira 517 (AD 1123); in science he was unrivalled—the very paragon of his age. Khwájah Nizámi of Samarcand who was one of his pupils, relates the following story:

"I often used to hold conversations with my teacher, Omar Khayyám, in a garden; and one day he said to me,

'my tomb shall be in a spot, where the north wind may scatter roses over it.'

I wondered at the words he spake, but I knew that his were no idle words.[3] Years after,

---

2 "Philosophe Musulman qui a vécu en Odeur de Sainteté dans la Fin du premier et le Commencement du second Siécle", no part of which, exccpt the "Philosophe", can apply to *our* Khayyám.

3 The Rashness of the Words, according to D'Herbelot, consisted in being so opposed to those in the Korán: " No man knows where he shall die."—This Story of Omar recalls a very different one so naturally—and, when one remembers how wide of his humble mark the noble sailor aimed—so pathetically told by Captain Cook—not by Doctor Hawkesworth—in his Second Voyage. When leaving Ulietea, "Oreo's last request was for me to return, when he saw that he could not obtain that promise, he asked the name of my *Marai*—Burying-place. As strange a question as this

when I chanced to revisit Naishápúr, I went to his final resting place, and lo! it was just outside a garden, and trees laden with fruit stretched their boughs over the garden wall, and dropped their flowers upon his tomb, so as the stone was hidden under them.""

Thus far-without fear of Trespass—from the *Calcutta Review*. The writer of it, on reading in India this story of Omar's Grave, was reminded, he says, of Cicero's Account of finding Archimedes' Tomb at Syracuse, buried in grass and weeds. I think Thorwaldsen desired to have roses grow over him; a wish religiously fulfilled for him to the present day, I believe. However, to return to Omar.

Though the Sultan "shower'd Favours upon him," Omar's Epicurean Audacity of Thought and Speech caused him to be regarded askance in his own Time and Country. He is said to have been especially hated and dreaded by the Súfis, whose Practice he ridiculed, and whose Faith amounts to little more than his own when stript of the Mysticism and formal recognition of Islamism under which

---

was, I hesitated not a moment to tell him, 'Stepney', the parish in which I live when in London. I was made to repeat it several times over until they could pronounce it.; and then 'Stepney Marai no Tootee' was echoed through a hundred mouths at once. I afterwards found that the same question had been put to Mr. Forster by a man on shore; but he gave a different, and indeed more proper answer, by saying, 'No man who used the sea could say where he should be buried'".

Omar would not hide. Their Poets, including Háfiz, who are (with the exception of Firdausi) the most considerable in Persia, borrowed largely, indeed, of Omar's material, but turning it to a mystical Use more convenient to Themselves and the People they addressed; a People quite as quick of Doubt as of Belief ; as keen of Bodily Sense as of Intellectual; and delighting in a cloudy compound of both, in which they could float luxuriously between Heaven and Earth, and this World and the Next, on the wings of a poetical expression, that might serve indifferently for either. Omar was too honest of Heart as well as of Head for this. Having failed (however mistakenly) of finding any Providence but Destiny, and any World but This, he set about making the most of it; preferring rather to soothe the Soul through the Senses into Acquiescence with Things as he saw them, than to perplex it with vain disquietude after what they *might be*. It has been seen, however, that his Worldly Ambition was not exorbitant; and he very likely takes a humorous or perverse pleasure in exalting the gratification of Sense above that of the intellect, in which he must have taken great delight, although it failed to answer the Questions in which he, in common with all men, was most vitally interested.

For whatever Reason, however, Omar, as before said, has never been popular in his own Country, and therefore has been but scantily transmitted abroad.

The MSS of his Poems, mutilated beyond the average Casualties of Oriental Transcription, are so rare in the East as scarce to have reacht Westward at all, in spite of all the acquisitions of Arms and Science. There is no copy at the India House, none at the Bibliothèque Impériale of Paris. We know but of one in England: No. 140 of the Ouseley MSS at the Bodleian, written at Shiraz, AD 1460. This contains but 158 Rubáiyát. One in the Asiatic Society's Library at Calcutta (of which we have a copy), contains (and yet incomplete) 516, though swelled to that by all kinds of Repetition and Corruption. So Von Hammer speaks of his Copy as containing about 200, while Dr. Sprenger catalogues the Lucknow MS at double that Number.[4] The Scribes too, of the Oxford and Calcutta MSS seem to do their work under a sort of Protest; each beginning with a Tetrastich (whether genuine or not), taken out of its alphabetic order; the Oxford with one of Apology; the Calcutta with one of Expostulation, supposed (says a notice prefixed to the MS) to have risen from a Dream, in which Omar's mother asked about his future fate. It may be rendered thus:—

4　"Since this Paper was written" (adds the Reviewer in a note) " we have met with a Copy of a very rare Edition, printed at Calcutta in 1836. This contains 438 Tetrastichs, with an Appendix containing 54 others not found in some MSS."

OH Thou who burn'st in Heart for those
who burn
In Hell, whose fires thyself shall feed in turn;
How long be crying, "Mercy on them, God!"
Why, who art Thou to teach, and He to learn?

The Bodleian Quatrain pleads Pantheism by way of
Justification.

IF I myself upon a looser Creed
Have loosely strung the Jewel of Good deed,
Let this one thing for my Atonement plead:
That One for Two I never did mis-read.

The Reviewer, to whom I owe the Particulars of
Omar's Life, concludes his Review by comparing
him with Lucretius, both as to natural Temper and
Genius, and as acted upon by the Circumstances
in which he lived. Both indeed were men of subtle,
strong, and cultivated Intellect, fine Imagination,
and Hearts passionate for Truth and Justice; who
justly revolted from their Country's false Religion,
and false, or foolish, Devotion to it; but who yet
fell short of replacing what they subverted by such
better *Hope* as others, with no better Revelation
to guide them, had yet made a Law to themselves.
Lucretius, indeed, with such material as Epicurus
furnished, satisfied himself with the theory of so vast
a machine fortuitously constructed, and acting by a

Law that implied no Legislator; and so composing himself into a Stoical rather than Epicurean severity of Attitude, sat down to contemplate the mechanical Drama of the Universe which he was part Actor in; himself and all about him (as in his own sublime description of the Roman Theatre) discoloured with the lurid reflex of the Curtain suspended between the Spectator and the Sun. Omar, more desperate, or more careless of any so complicated system as resulted in nothing but hopeless Necessity, flung his own Genius and Learning with a bitter or humorous jest into the general Ruin which their insufficient glimpses only served to reveal; and, pretending sensual pleasure as the serious purpose of Life, only *diverted* himself with speculative problems of Deity, Destiny, Matter and Spirit, Good and Evil, and other such questions, easier to start than to run down, and the pursuit of which becomes a very weary sport at last!

With regard to the present Translation. The original Rubáiyát (as, missing an Arabic Guttural, these *Tetrastichs* are more musically called) are independent Stanzas, consisting each of four Lines of equal, though varied, Prosody; sometimes *all* rhyming, but oftener (as here imitated) the third line a blank. Something as in the Greek Alcaic, where the penultimate line seems to lift and suspend the Wave that falls over in the last. As usual with such kind of Oriental Verse, the Rubáiyát follow one another according to Alphabetic Rhyme—a strange succession of Grave and Gay. Those here selected are strung into something of an Eclogue, with perhaps less than equal proportion of the "Drink and make-merry", which (genuine or not) recurs over-frequently in the Original. Either way, the Result is sad enough: saddest perhaps when most ostentatiously merry: more apt to move Sorrow than Anger toward the old Tent-maker, who, after vainly endeavouring to unshackle his Steps from Destiny, and to catch some authentic Glimpse of TO-MORROW, fell back upon TO-DAY (which has outlasted so many TO-MORROWS!) as the only Ground he got to stand upon, however momentarily slipping from under his Feet.

While the present Edition of Omar was preparing, Monsieur Nicolas, French Consul at Rescht, published a very careful and very good Edition of the Text, from a lithograph copy at Teheran, comprising 464 Rubáiyát, with translation and notes of his own.

Mons. Nicolas, whose Edition has reminded me of several things, and instructed me in others, does not consider Omar to be the material Epicurean that I have literally taken him for, but a Mystic, shadowing the Deity under the figure of Wine, Wine-bearer, etc., as Háfiz is supposed to do; in short, a Súfi Poet like Háfiz and the rest.

I cannot see reason to alter my opinion, formed as it was a dozen years ago when Omar was first shown me by one to whom I am indebted for all I know of Oriental, and very much of other, literature. He admired Omar's Genius so much, that he would gladly have adopted any such Interpretation of his meaning as Mons. Nicolas if he could.[5] That he could not appears by his Paper in the *Calcutta Review* already so largely quoted; in which he argues from the Poems themselves, as well as from what records remain the Poet's Life.

And if more were needed to disprove Mons. Nicolas' Theory, there is the Biographical Notice which he himself has drawn up in direct contradiction to the Interpretation of the Poems given in his Notes. Here is one of the Anecdotes he produces.

"Mais ravenons à Khéyam, qui, resté étranger à toutes ces alternatives de guerres, d'intrigues, et de révoltes, dont cette époque fut si remplie, vivait tranquille dans son village natal, se livrant avec passion à l'étude de la philosophie des Soufis. Entouré de nombreux amis il cherchait avec eux dans le vin cette contemplation extatique que d'autres croient trouver dans des cris et des hurlemens," etc. "Les chroniqueurs

---

5 Perhaps would have edited the poem himself some years ago. He may now as little approve of my Version on one-side, as of Mons. Nicolas' on the other.

persans racontent que Khéyam aimait surtout à s'entretenir at à boire avec ses amis, le soir au clair de la lune sur la terrasse de se maison, entouré de chanteurs et musiciens, avec un échanson qui, la coupe à la main, la présentait à tour de rôle aux joyeux convives réunis.—Pendant une de ces soirées dont nousvenons de parler, survient à l'improviste un coup de vent qui éteint les chandelles et renverse à terre la cruche de vin, placée imprudemment sur le bord de la terrasse. La cruche fut brisée et le vin repandu. Aussitôt Khéyam, irrité, improvisa ce quatrain impie à l'adresse du Tout-Puissant: 'Tu as brisé ma cruche de vin, mon Dieu! tu as ainsi fermé sur moi la porte de la joie, mon Dieu! c'est moi qui bois, et c'est toi qui commets les désordres de l'ivresse! oh! (puisse ma bouche se remplir de la terre!) serais-tu ivre, mon Dieu!'

"Le poéte, aprés avoir prononcé ce blasphéme, jetant les yeux sur une glace, se serait aperçu que son visage était noir comme du charbon. C'était une punition du ciel. Alors il fit cet autre quatrain non moins audacieux que le premier. 'Quel est l'homme ici-bas qui n'a point commis de péche, dis? Celui qui n'en aurait point commis, comment aurait-il vécu, dis? Si, parce que je fais du mal, tu me punis par le mal, quelle est donc la différence qui existe entre toi et moi, dis?'"

I really hardly knew poor Omar was so far gone till his Apologist informed me. Here we see then that, whatever were the Wine that Háfiz drank and sang, the veritable Juice of the Grape it was which Omar used not only when carousing with his friends, but (says Mons. Nicolas) in order to excite himself to that pitch of Devotion which others reached by cries and "hurlemens" and yet, whenever Wine, Wine-bearer' etc., occur in the Text—which is often enough—Mons. Nicolas carefully annotates "Dieu", "La Divinité", etc.; so carefully indeed that one is tempted to think he was indoctrinated by the Súfi with whom he read the Poems. (Note to Rub. ii. p. 8) A Persian would naturally wish to vindicate a distinguished Countryman; and a Súfi to enrol him in his own sect, which already comprises all the chief Poets of Persia.

What historical Authority has Mons. Nicolas to show that Omar gave himself up "avec passion à l'étude de la philosophie des Soufis"? (Preface, p.xiii.) The Doctrines of Pantheism, Materialism, Necessity, etc., were not peculiar to the Súfi; nor to Lucretius before them; nor to Epicurus before him; probably the very original Irreligion of thinking men from the first; and very likely to be the spontaneous growth of a Philosopher living in an Age of social and political barbarism, under sanction of one of the Two and Seventy Religions supposed to divide the world. Von Hammer (according to Sprenger's

Oriental Catalogue) speaks of Omar as "a Free-thinker, and *a great opponent of Súfism*", perhaps because, while holding much of their Doctrine, he would not pretend to any inconsistent severity of morals. Sir W. Ouseley has written a Note to something of the same effect on the flyleaf of the Bodleian MS. And in two Rubáiyát of Mons. Nicolas' own Edition Súf and Súfi are both disparagingly named.

No doubt many of these Quatrains seem unaccountable unless mystically interpreted; but many more as unaccountable unless literally. Were the Wine spiritual, for instance, how wash the Body with it when dead? Why make cups of the dead clay to be filled with—"La Divinité"—by some succeeding Mystic? Mons. Nicolas himself is puzzled by some "bizarres" and "trop Orientales" allusions and images—"d'une sensualité quelquefois révoltante" indeed—which "les convenances" do not perrnit him to translate; but still which the reader cannot but refer to "La Divinité"[6] No doubt also many of the Quatrains in the Teheran, as in the Calcutta, Copies, are spurious; such Rubáiyát being the common form of Epigram in Persia. But this, at best, tells as much one way as another; nay, the Súfi, who may be considered the Scholar and Man of Letters in Persia, would be far more likely than the careless Epicure to interpolate what favours his own view of the Poet. I observe that very few of the more mystical Quatrains are in the Bodleian MS, which must be one of the oldest, as dated at Shiraz, AH 865, AD 1460. And this, I think, especially distinguishes Omar (I cannot help calling him by his—no, not Christian—familiar name) from all other Persian Poets: That, whereas with them the Poet is lost in his Song, the Man in Allegory and Abstraction; we seem to have the Man—the *Bonhomme*—Omar himself, with all his Humours and Passions, as frankly before us as if we were really at Table with him, after the Wine had gone round.

I must say that I, for one, never wholly believed in the Mysticism of Háfiz. It does not appear there was any danger in holding and singing Súfi Pantheism, so long as the Poet made his Salaam to Mohammed at the beginning and end of his Song. Under such conditions Jeláluddín, Jámi, Attár, and others sang; using Wine and Beauty indeed as Images to illustrate, not as a Mask to hide, the Divinity they were celebrating. Perhaps some Allegory less liable to mistake or abuse had been better among so inflammable a People: much more so when, as some think with Háfiz and Omar, the abstract is not only likened to, but identified with, the sensual Image; hazardous, if not to the Devotee himself, yet to his weaker Brethren; and worse for the Profane in proportion as the Devotion of the Initiated grew warmer. And all for what? To be tantalised with Images of sensual enjoyment which must be renounced if one would approximate a God, who, according to the Doctrine, *is* Sensual Matter as well as Spirit, and into whose Universe one expects unconsciously to merge after Death, without hope of any posthumous Beatitude in another world to compensate for all the self-denial of this. Lucretius' blind Divinity certainly merited, and probably got, as much self-sacrifice as this of the Súfi; and the burden of Omar's Song—if not "Let us eat"—is assuredly—"Let us drink, for To-morrow we die!" And if Háfiz meant quite otherwise by a similar language, he surely miscalculated when he devoted his Life and Genius to so equivocal a Psalmody as, from his Day to this, has been said and sung by any rather than spiritual Worshippers.

However, it may remain an Open Question, both with regard to Háfiz and Omar: the reader may understand them either way, literally or mystically, as he chooses. Whenever Wine, Wine-bearer, Cypress, etc.' are named, he has only to suppose "La Divinité"; and when he has done so with Omar, I really think he may proceed to the same Interpretation of Anacreon—and even Anacreon Moore.

Rubáiyát

of

Omar Khayyám

Second Edition, 1868

I

WAKE! For the Sun behind yon
    Eastern height
Has chased the Session of the Stars
    from Night;
And, to the field of Heav'n ascending,
    strikes
The Sultán's Turret with a Shaft of
    Light

II

Before the phantom of False
    morning died,
Methought a Voice within the Tavern
    cried,
"When all the Temple is prepared
    within,
Why lags the drowsy Worshipper
    outside!"

III

AND, as the Cock crew, those who stood before
The Tavern shouted—"Open then the
    door!
You know how little while we have
    to stay,
And, once departed, may return no
    more."

IV

NOW the New Year reviving old Desires,
The thoughtful Soul to Solitude
    retires,
Where the WHITE HAND OF MOSES
    on the Bough
Puts out, and Jesus from the ground
    suspires

V

IRAM indeed is gone with all his
    Rose,
And Jamshýd's Sev'n-ring'd Cup
    where no one knows;
But still a Ruby gushes from the
    Vine,
And many a Garden by the Water
    blows'

VI

AND David's lips are lockt; but in
    divine
High-piping Péhlevi, with "Wine!
    Wine! Wine!
Red Wine!"—the Nightingale cries to
    the Rose
That sallow cheek of hers to
    incarnadine

VII

COME, fill the Cup, and in the
fire of Spring
Your Winter-garment of Repentance
    fling:
The Bird of Time has but a little
    way
To flutter—and the Bird is on the
    wing

VIII

WHETHER at Naishápúr or
Babylon,
Whether the Cup with sweet or bitter
    run
The Wine of Life keeps oozing drop
    by drop,
The Leaves of Life keep falling one
    by one.

IX

MORNING, a thousand Roses
brings, you say;
Yes, but where leaves the Rose of
yesterday?
And this first Summer month that
brings the Rose
Shall take Jamshýd and Kaikobád
away.

X

WELL, let it take them ! What
have we to do
With Kaikobád the Great, or
Kaikhosrú
Let Rustum cry "To Battle!" as he
likes,
Or Hátim Tai "To Supper!"—heed
not you.

XI

WITH me along the strip of
    Herbage strown
That just divides the desert from the
    sown,
Where name of Slave and Sultán is
    forgot—
And Peace to Máhmúd on his golden
    Throne !

XII

HERE with a little Bread beneath
    the Bough,
A Flask of Wine, a Book of Verse—
    and Thou
Beside me singing in the
    Wilderness—
Oh, Wilderness were Paradise
    enow!

XIII

SOME for the Glories of This
World; and some
Sigh for the Prophet's Paradise to
   come;
Ah, take the Cash, and let the
   Promise go.
Nor heed the music of a distant
   Drum!

XIV

WERE it not Folly, Spider-like to
   spin
The Thread of present Life away to
   win—
What? for ourselves, who know not if
   we shall
Breathe out the very Breath we now
   breathe in!

XV

LOOK to the blowing Rose about us—, "Lo,
Laughing," she says, "into the world I
    blow:
At once the silken tassel of my Purse
Tear, and its Treasure on the Garden
    throw."

XVI

FOR those who husbanded the
    Golden grain,
And those who flung it to the winds
    like Rain,
Alike to no such aureate Earth are
    turn'd
As, buried once, Men want dug up
    again.

XVII

THE Worldly Hope men set their
  Hearts upon
Turns Ashes—or it prospers; and
  anon,
Like Snow upon the Desert's dusty
  Face,
Lighting a little hour or two—was
  gone.

XVIII

THINK, in this batter'd
  Caravanserai
Whose Portals are alternate Night
  and Day,
How Sultán after Sultán with his
  Pomp
Abode his destin'd Hour, and went
  his way.

XIX

THEY say the Lion and the Lizard keep
The Courts where Jamshýd gloried
  and drank deep:
And Bahrám, that great Hunter—the
  Wild Ass
Stamps o'er his Head, but cannot
  break his Sleep.

XX

THE Palace that to Heav'n his
  pillars I threw,
And Kings the forehead on his
  threshold drew—
I saw the solitary Ringdove there,
And "Coo, coo, coo," she cried; and
  "Coo, coo, coo."

XXI

AH, my Belovéd, fill the Cup that clears
To-DAY of past Regret and future
  Fears:
To-morrow!—Why, To-morrow I
  may be
Myself with Yesterday's Sev'n
  thousand Years.

XXII

FOR some we loved, the loveliest
  and the best
That from his Vintage rolling Time
  has prest,
Have drunk their Cup a Round or
  two before,
And one by one crept silently to rest.

XXIII

AND we, that now make merry in the Room
They left, and Summer dresses in new
   bloom,
Ourselves must beneath the Couch
   of Earth
Descend, ourselves to make a
   Couch—for whom?

XXIV

I SOMETIMES think that never blows so red
The Rose as where some buried
   Cæsar bled;
That every Hyacinth the Garden
   wears
Dropt in her lap from some once
   lovely Head.

XXV

AND this delightful Herb whose living Green
Fledges the River's Lip on which we
    lean—
Ah, lean upon it lightly! for who
    knows
From what once lovely Lip it springs
    unseen!

XXVI

AH, make the most of what we Yet
    may spend,
Before we too into the Dust descend;
Dust into Dust, and under Dust, to
    lie,
Sans Wine, sans Song sans Singer,
    and—sans End!

XXVII

ALIKE for those who for TO-DAY prepare,
And those that after some To-
  MORROW stare,
A Muezzín from the Tower of
  Darkness cries,
"Fools! your Reward is neither Here
  nor There!"

XXVIII

ANOTHER Voice, when I am
  sleeping cries,
"The Flower should open with the
  Morning skies."
and a retreating Whisper, as I wake—
"The Flower that once has blown for
  ever dies."

XXIX

WHY, all the Saints and Sages who discuss'd
Of the Two Worlds so learnedly, are thrust
   Like foolish Prophets forth; their Words to Scorn
Are scatter'd, and their Mouths are stopt with Dust.

XXX

MYSELF when young did eagerly frequent
Doctor and Saint, and heard great argument
   About it and about: but evermore
Came out by the same door as in I went.

XXXI

WITH them the seed of Wisdom did I sow,
And with my own hand wrought to make it grow:
And this was all the Harvest that I reap'd—
"I came like Water, and like Wind I go."

XXXII

INTO this Universe, and *Why* not knowing,
Nor *Whence*, like Water willy-nilly flowing:
And out of it, as Wind along the Waste,
I know not *whither*, willy-nilly blowing.

XXXIII

WHAT, without asking, hither
 hurried *Whence?*
And, without asking, *Whither* hurried
 hence!
Ah, contrite Heav'n endowed us with
 the Vine
To drug the memory of that
 insolence!

XXXIV

UP from Earth's Centre through
 the Seventh Gate
I rose, and on the Throne of Saturn
 sate,
And many Knots unravel'd by the
 Road;
But not the Master-knot of Human
 Fate.

XXXV

THERE was the Door to which I found no Key:
There was the Veil through which I
    could not see:
Some little talk awhile of ME and
    THEE
There was—and then no more of
    THEE and ME.

XXXVI

EARTH could not answer: nor the Seas that mourn
In flowing Purple, of their Lord
    forlorn;
Nor Heaven, with those eternal Signs
    reveal'd
And hidden by the sleeve of Night
    and Morn.

XXXVII

THEN of THEE IN ME who works behind
The Veil of Universe I cried to find
A Lamp to guide me through the
    darkness; and
Something then said—"an
    Understanding blind."

XXXVIII

THEN to the Lip of this poor earthen Urn
I lean'd, the secret Well of Life to
    learn:
And Lip to Lip it murmur'd—"While
    you live,
Drink!—for, once dead, you never
    shall return."

XXXIX

I THINK the Vessel, that with fugitive
Articulation answer'd, once did
    live,
And drink; and that impassive Lip I
    kiss'd,
How many Kisses might it take—and
    give!

XL

FOR I remember stopping by the
    way
To watch a Potter thumping his wet
    Clay:
And with its all-obliterated Tongue
It murmur'd—"Gently, Brother,
    gently, pray!"

XLI

FOR has not such a Story from of
Old
Down Man's successive generations
roll'd
Of such a clod of saturated Earth
Cast by the Maker into Human
mould?

XLII

AND not a drop that from our
Cups we throw
On the Parcht herbage but may steal
below
To quench the fire of Anguish in some
Eye
There hidden—far beneath, and long
ago.

XLIII

A S then the Tulip for her wonted sup
Of Heavenly Vintage lifts her
    chalice up,
Do you, twin offspring of the soil, till
    Heav'n
To Earth invert you like an empty
    Cup.

XLIV

D O you, within your little hour of
    Grace,
The waving Cypress in your Arms
    enlace,
Before the Mother back into her
    arms
Fold, and dissolve you in a last
    embrace

XLV

AND if the Cup you drink, the Lip
  you press,
End in what All begins and ends
  in—Yes;
Imagine then you *are* what
  heretofore
You *were*—hereafter you shall not
  be less.

XLVI

SO when at last the Angel of the
  drink
Of Darkness finds you by the river-
  brink
And, proffering his Cup, invites your
  Soul
Forth to your Lips to quaff it—do
  not shrink

XLVII

AND fear not lest Existence closing *your*
Account, should lose, or know the
    type no more;
The Eternal Sáki from that Bowl has
    pour'd
Millions of Bubbles like us, and will
    pour.

XLVIII

WHEN You and I behind the Veil
    are Past,
Oh but the long long while the World
    shall last,
Which of our Coming and Departure
heeds
As much as Ocean of a pebble-cast.

IL

ONE Moment in Annihilation's
Waste,
One Moment, of the Well of Life to
taste—
The Stars are setting, and the
Caravan
Draws to the Dawn of Nothing—Oh
make haste!

L

WOULD you that spangle of
Existence spend
About THE SECRET—quick about it,
Friend!
A Hair, they say, divides the False
from the True—
And upon what, prithee, does Life
depend?

LI

A HAIR, they say divides the False
and True;
Yes; and a single Alif were the clue,
Could you but find it, to the
Treasure-house.
And peradventure to THE MASTER
too;

LII

WHOSE secret Presence, through
Creation's veins
Running, Quicksilver-like eludes your
pains:
Taking all shapes from Máh to
Máhi; and
They change and perish all—but He
remains;

LIII

A MOMENT guess'd—then back
behind the Fold
Immerst of Darkness round the
Drama roll'd
Which, for the Pastime of Eternity,
He does Himself contrive, enact,
behold.

LIV

BUT if in vain, down on the
stubborn floor
Of Earth, and up to Heav'n's
unopened Door,
You gaze To-day, while You are
You—how then
To-morrow, You when shall be You
no more?

LV

OH, plagued no more with
Human or Divine,
To-morrow's tangle to itself resign,
And lose your fingers in the tresses
    of
The Cypress-slender Minister of
    Wine.

LVI

WASTE not your Hour, not in
the vain Pursuit
Of This and That endeavour and
    dispute;
Better be merry with the fruitful
    Grape
Than sadden after none, or bitter,
    Fruit.

LVII

YOU know my Friends, how
bravely in my House
For a new Marriage I did make
  Carouse:
Divorced old barren Reason from my
  Bed,
And took the Daughter of the Vine to
  Spouse.

LVIII

FOR "Is" and "Is-not" though
with Rule and Line
And "Up-and-down" by Logic I
  define,
of all that one should care fathom I,
Was never deep in anything but—
  Wine.

LIX

AH, but my Computations, People
    say,
Have squared the Year to human
    compass, eh?
If so, by striking from the Calendar
Unborn To-morrow, and dead
    Yesterday.

LX

AND lately, by the Tavern Door
    agape,
Came shining through the Dusk an
    Angel Shape
Bearing a Vessel on his Shoulder; and
He bid me taste of it; and 'twas—the
    Grape!

LXI

THE Grape that can with Logic absolute
The Two-and-Seventy jarring Sects confute:
The sovereign Alchemist that in a trice
Life's leaden metal into Gold transmute:

LXII

THE mighty Mahmúd, Allah-breathing Lord,
That all the misbelieving and black Horde
Of Fears and Sorrows that infest the Soul
Scatters before him with his whirlwind Sword.

LXIII

WHY, be this Juice the growth of God, who dare
Blaspheme the twisted tendril as a
    Snare?
A Blessing, we should use it, should
    we not?
And if a Curse—why, then, who set it
    there?

LXIV

I must abjure the Balm of Life, I
    must,
Scared by some After-reckoning ta'en
    on trust,
Or lured with Hope of some Diviner
    Drink
When the frail Cup is crumbled into
    Dust?

LXV

IF but the Vine and Love-abjuring
   Band
Are in the Prophet's Paradise to
   stand,
Alack, I doubt the Prophet's
   Paradise
Were empty as the hollow of one's
   Hand.

LXVI

OH threats of Hell and Hopes of
   Paradise!
One thing at least is certain—*This*
   Life flies:
One thing is certain and the rest is
   Lies;
The Flower that once is Blown for
   ever dies.

LXVII

STRANGE, is it not? that of the
myriads who
Before us pass'd the door of Darkness
through
Not one returns to tell us of the
Road,
Which to discover we must travel
too.

LXVIII

THE Revelations of Devout and
Learn'd
Who rose before us, and as Prophets
burn'd,
Are all but Stories, which, awoke
from Sleep
They told their fellows, and to Sleep
return'd.

LXIX

WHY, if the Soul can fling the
    Dust aside,
And naked on the Air of Heaven
    ride,
Is't not a shame—is't not a shame for
    him
So long in this Clay suburb to abide!

LXX

BUT that is but a Tent wherin may
    rest
A Sultan to the realm of Death
    addrest;
The Sultan rises, and the dark
    Ferrásh
Strikes, and prepares it for another
    guest.

LXXI

I SENT my Soul through the
Invisible,
Some letter of that Afterlife to spell:
And after many days my Soul
    return'd
And said, "Behold, Myself am Heav'n
    and Hell:"

LXXII

HEAV'N but the Vision of fulfill'd
Desire,
And Hell the Shadow of a Soul on
    fire,
Cast on the Darkness into which
    Ourselves,
So late emerg'd from, shall so soon
    expire.

LXXIII

WE are no other than a moving row
Of visionary Shapes that come and go
Round with this Sun-illumin'd
    Lantern held
In Midnight by the Master of the
    Show;

LXXIV

IMPOTENT Pieces of the Game he
    plays
Upon this Chequer-board of Nights
    and Days;
Hither and thither moves, checks and
    slays;
And one by one back in the Closet
    lays.

LXXV

THE Ball no question makes of Ayes and Noes,
But Right or Left as strikes the Player
  goes;
And He that toss'd you down into
  the Field,
He knows about it all—HE knows—
  HE knows!

LXXVI

THE Moving Finger writes; and,
  having writ,
Moves on: nor all your Piety nor
  Wit
Shall lure it back to cancel half a
  Line,
Nor all your Tears wash out a
  Word of it.

LXXVII

FOR let Philosopher and Doctor
    preach
Of what they will, and what they will
    not—each
Is but one Link in an eternal Chain
That none can slip, nor break, nor
    overreach.

LXXVIII

AND that inverted Bowl we call
    The Sky,
Whereunder crawling coop'd we
    live and die,
Lift not your hands to *It* for help—
    for It
As impotently rolls as you or I.

LXXIX

WITH Earth's first Clay They did
    the Last Man knead,
And there of the Last Harvest sow'd
    the Seed:
And the first Morning of Creation
    wrote
What the Last Dawn of Reckoning
    shall read.

LXXX

YESTERDAY *This* Day's Madness
    did I prepare:
To-morrow's Silence, Triumph, or
    Despair:
Drink! for you know not whence you
    came, nor why;
Drink! for you know not why you go,
    nor where.

LXXXI

I TELL you this—When, started from the Goal,
Over the flaming shoulders of the
    Foal
Of Heav'n Parwín and Mushtari they
    flung
In my predestin'd Plot of Dust and
    Soul.

LXXXII

THE Vine had struck a fibre: which about
If clings my being—let the Dervish
    flout;
Of my Base metal may be filed a Key,
That shall unlock the Door he howls
    without.

LXXXIII

AND this I know: whether the one True Light,
Kindle to Love, or Wrath-consume me quite,
  One Flash of It within the Tavern caught
Better than in the Temple lost outright.

LXXXIV

WHAT! out of senseless Nothing to provoke
A conscious Something to resent the yoke
  Of unpermitted Pleasure, under pain
Of Everlasting Penalties, if broke!

LXXXV

WHAT! from his helpless
  Creature be repaid
Pure Gold for what he lent us dross-
  allay'd—
Sue for a Debt we never did
  contract,
And cannot answer—Oh the sorry
  trade!

LXXXVI

NAY, but, for terror of his
  wrathful Face,
I swear I will not call Injustice
  Grace;
Not one Good Fellow of the Tavern
  but
Would kick so poor a Coward from
  the place.

LXXXVII

OH Thou, who didst with pitfall and with gin
Beset the Road I was to wander in,
Thou wilt not with Predestin'd Evil round
  Enmesh, and then impute my Fall to
  Sin?

LXXXVIII

OH Thou, who Man of baser Earth didst make,
And ev'n with Paradise devise the
  Snake:
For all the Sin the Face of wretched
  Man
Is black with—Man's Forgiveness
  give—and take!

LXXXIX

AS under cover of departing Day
Slunk hunger-stricken Ramazán
   away,
Once more within the Potter's house
   alone
I stood, surrounded by the Shapes of
   Clay.

XC

AND once again there gather'd a
   scarce heard
Whisper among them; as it were, the
stirr'd
Ashes of some all but extinguisht
   Tongue,
Which mine ear kindled into living
   Word.

XCI

SAID one among them—"Surely not in vain,
My substance from the common
    Earth was ta'en,
That He who subtly wrought me into
    Shape
Should stamp me back to shapeless
    Earth again?"

XCII

ANOTHER said—"Why, ne'er a peevish Boy
Would break the Cup from which he
    drank in Joy;
Shall He that of his own free Fancy
    made
The Vessel, in an after-rage destroy!"

XCIII

NONE answer'd this; but after silence spake
Some Vessel of a more ungainly
   Make;
"They sneer at me for leaning all
   awry:
What! did the Hand then of the
   Potter shake?"

XCIV

THUS with the Dead as with the
   Living, *What*?
And *Why*? so ready, but the
   Wherefor not,
One on a sudden peevishly
   exclaim'd,
"Which is the Potter, pray, and
   which the Pot?"

XCV

SAID one—"Folks of a surly Master tell,
And daub his Visage with the Smoke
of Hell:
They talk of some sharp Trial of us—
Pish!
He's a Good Fellow, and 'twill all be
well."

XCVI

"WELL," said, another, "whoso
will, let try
My Clay with long oblivion is gone
dry:
But fill me with the old familiar
Juice,
Methinks I might recover by-and-
bye!"

XCVII

SO while the Vessels one by one
were speaking,
One spied the little Crescent all were
seeking:
And then they jogged each other,
"Brother! Brother!
Now for the Porter's shoulder-knot
a-creaking!"

XCVIII

AH, with the Grape my fading life
provide,
And wash my Body whence the Life
has died,
And lay me shrouded in the living
Leaf,
By some not unfrequented Garden-
side.

XCIX

WHITHER resorting from the
vernal Heat
Shall Old Acquaintance Old
  Acquaintance greet,
Under the Branch that leans above
  the Wall
To shed his Blossom over head and
  feet.

C

THEN ev'n my buried Ashes such
  a snare
Of Vintage shall fling up into the
  Air.
As not a true-believer passing by
But shall be overtaken unaware.

CI

INDEED the Idols I have loved so
  long
Have done my credit in Men's eye
  much wrong:
Have drown'd my Glory in a shallow
  Cup,
And sold my Reputation for a Song.

CII

INDEED, indeed, Repentence oft
  before
I swore—but was I sober when I
  swore?
And then and then came Spring, and
  Rose-in-hand
My thread-bare Penitence apieces
  tore.

CIII

AND much as Wine has played the
Infidel,
And robb'd me of my Robe of
    Honour—Well,
I often wonder what the Vintners
    buy
One half so precious as the ware they
sell.

CIV

YET Ah, that Spring should vanish
    with the Rose!
That Youth's sweet-scented
    manuscript should close!
The Nightingale that in the branches
    sang,
Ah whence, and whither flown again,
    who knows!

CV

WOULD but the Desert of the
    Fountain yield
One glimpse—if dimly, yet indeed
    reveal'd,
Toward which the fainting Traveller
    might spring,
As springs the trampled herbage of
    the field!

CVI

OH if the World were but to re-
    create,
That we might catch ere closed the
    Book of Fate,
And make The Writer on a fairer
    leaf.
Inscribe our names, or quite
    obliterate!

CVII

BETTER, oh better, cancel from the Scroll
Of Universe one luckless Human
    Soul,
Than drop by drop enlarge the Flood
    that rolls
Hoarser with Anguish as the Ages
    roll.

CVIII

AH Love! could you and I with
    Fate conspire
To grasp this sorry Scheme of Things
    entire,
Would not we shatter it to bits—and
    then
Re-mould it nearer to the Heart's
    Desire!

CIX

BUT see! The rising Moon of
Heav'n again
Looks for us, Sweet-heart, through
   the quivering Plane:
How oft hereafter rising will she look
Among those leaves—for one of us in
   vain!

CX

AND when Yourself with silver
Foot shall pass
Among the Guests Star-scatter' d on
   the Grass,
And in your joyous errand reach the
   spot
Where I made One—turn down an
   empty Glass!

TÁMÁM.

Preface to the third edition, 1872

WHILE the second Edition of this version of Omar was preparing, Monsieur Nicolas, French Consul at Resht, published a very careful and very good Edition of the Text, from a lithograph copy at Teheran, comprising 464 *Rubáiyát*, with translation and notes of his own.

Mons. Nicolas, whose Edition has reminded me of several things, and instructed me in others, does not consider Omar to be the material Epicurean that I have literally taken him for, but a Mystic, shadowing the Deity under the figure of Wine, Wine-bearer, &c., as Háfiz is supposed to do; in short, a Súfi poet like Háfiz and the rest.

I cannot see reason to alter my opinion, formed as it was more than a dozen years ago (1868) when Omar was first shown me by one to whom I am indebted for all I know of Oriental, and very much of other, literature. He admired Omar's Genius so much, that he would gladly have adopted any such Interpretation of his meaning as Mons. Nicolas' if he could.[1] That he could not, appears by his Paper in the *Calcutta Review* already so largely quoted; in

---

[1] Perhaps would have edited the Poems himself some years ago. He may now as little approve, of my Version on one side, as of Mons. Nicolas' Theory on the other.

which he argues from the Poems themselves, as well as from what records remain of the Poet's Life. And if more were needed to disprove Mons. Nicolas' Theory, there is the Biographical Notice which he himself has drawn up in direct contradiction to the Interpretation of the Poems given in his Notes. (See pp xiii–xiv of his Preface.) Indeed I hardly knew poor Omar was so far gone till his Apologist informed me. For here we see that whatever were the Wine that Háfiz drank and sang, the veritable Juice of the Grape it was which Omar used, not only when carousing with his friends, but (say Mons. Nicolas) in order to excite himself to that pitch of Devotion which others reached by cries and *"hurlemens."* And yet, whenever Wine, Wine-bearer, &c., occur in the text—which is often enough—Mons. Nicolas carefully annotates *"Dieu" "La Divinité,"* &c.: so carefully indeed that one is tempted to think that he was indoctrinated by the Súfi with whom he read the Poems. (Note to Rub. ii. p. 8.) A Persian would naturally wish to vindicate a distinguished Countryman; and a Súfi to enrol him in his own sect, which already comprises all the chief Poets of Persia.

What historical Authority has Mons. Nicolas to show that Omar gave himself up *"avec passion à l'étude de la philosophie des Soufis?"* (Preface p. xiii) The Doctrines of Pantheism, Materialism, Necessity, &c., were not peculiar to the Súfi; nor to

Lucretius before them; nor to Epicurus before him; probably the very original Irreligion of Thinking men from the first; and very likely to be the spontaneous growth of a Philosopher living in an Age of social and political barbarism, under shadow of one of the Two and Seventy Religions supposed to divide the world. Von Hammer (according to Sprenger's Oriental Catalogue) speaks of Omar as "a Free-thinker, and *a great opponent of Súfism;*" perhaps because, while holding much of their Doctrine, he would not pretend to any inconsistent severity of morals. Sir W. Ouseley has written a note to something of the same effect on the fly-leaf of the Bodleian MS. And in two *Rubáiyát* of Mons. Nicolas' own Edition Suf and Súfi are both disparagingly named.

No doubt many of these Quatrains seem unaccountable unless mystically interpreted; but many more as unaccountable unless literally. Were the Wine spiritual, for instance, how wash the Body with it when dead? Why make cups of the dead clay to be filled with—"*La Divinité*"—by some succeeding Mystic? Mons. Nicolas himself is puzzled by some "*bizarres*" and "*trop Orientales*" allusions and images—"*d'une sensualité quelquefois révoltante*" indeed—which "*les covenances*" do not permit him to translate; but still which the reader cannot but refer to "*La Divinité.*"[2] No doubt

---

2 A Note to Quatrain 234 admits that, however clear the mystical

also many of the Quatrains in the Teheran, as in
the Calcutta, Copies, are spurious; such *Rubáiyát*
being the common form of Epigram in Persia. But
this, at best, tells as much one way as another;
nay, the Súfi, who may be considered the Scholar
and Man of Letters in Persia, would be far more
likely than the careless Epicure to interpolate what
favours his own view of the Poet. I observe that
very few of the more mystical Quatrains are in
the Bodleian MS. which must be one of the oldest,
as dated at Shiraz, AH 865, AD 1460. And this, I
think, especially distinguishes Omar (I cannot help
calling him by his—no, not Christian—familiar
name) from all other Persian Poets: That, whereas
with them the Poet is lost in his Song, the Man
in Allegory and Abstraction; we seem to have the
Man—the *Bonhomme*—Omar himself, with all his
Humours and Passions, as frankly before us as if
we were really at Table with him, after the Wine
had gone round. I must say that I, for one, never

meaning of such Images must be to Europeans, they are not
quoted without *"rougissant"* even by laymen in Persia—*"Quant
aux termes de tendresse qui commencent ce quatrain, comme
tant d'autres dans ce recueil, nos lecteurs, habitués maintenant
á l'étrangeté des expressions si souvant employées par Khéyam
pour rendre ses pensées sur l'amour divin, et á la singularité de ses
images trop orientales, d'une sensualité quelquefois révoltante,
n'auront pas de peine á se persuader qu'il s'agit de la Divinité,
bien qu cette conviction soit vivement discutée par les moullahs
musulmans et méme par beaucoup de laiqucs, qui rougissent
véritablement d'une pareille licence de leur compatriote á l'égard
des choses spiritualles."*

wholly believed in the Mysticism of Háfiz. It does not appear there was any danger in holding and singing Súfi Pantheism, so long as the Poet made his Salaam to Mohammed at the beginning and end of his Song. Under such conditions Jeláluddín, Jámi, Attár, and others sang; using Wine and Beauty indeed as Images to illustrate, not as a Mask to hide, the Divinity they were celebrating. Perhaps some Allegory less liable to mistake or abuse had been better among so inflammable a People: much more so when, as some think with Háfiz and Omar, the abstract is not only likened to, but identified with, the sensual Image; hazardous, if not to the Devotee himself, yet to his weaker Brethren; and worse for the Profane in proportion as the Devotion of the Initiated grew warmer. And all for what? To be tantalised with Images of sensual enjoyment which must be renounced if one would approximate a God, who according to the Doctrine, *is* Sensual Matter as well as Spirit, and into whose universe one expects unconsciously to merge after Death, without hope of any posthumous Beatitude in another world to compensate for all one's self-denial in this. Lucretius' blind Divinity certainly merited, and probably got, as much self-sacrifice as this of the Súfi; and the burden of Omar's Song—if not "Let us eat"—is assuredly—"Let us drink, for To-morrow we die!" And if Háfiz meant quite otherwise by a similar language, he surely miscalculated when he devoted his Life and Genius to so equivocal a Psalmody as, from his Day to this, has been said and sung by any rather than Spiritual Worshippers.

However, as there is some traditional presumption, and certainly. the opinion of some learned men, in favour of Omar's being a Súfi— and even something of a Saint—those who please may so interpret his Wine and Cup-bearer. On the other hand, as there is far more historical certainty of his being a Philosopher, of scientific Insight and Ability far beyond that of the Age and Country he lived in; of such moderate worldly Ambition as becomes a Philosopher, and such moderate wants as rarely satisfy a Debauchee: other readers may be content to believe with me that, while the Wine Omar celebrates is simply the Juice of the Grape, he bragged more than he drank of it, in very defiance perhaps of that Spiritual Wine which left its votaries sunk in Hypocrisy or Disgust

Edward FitzGerald

Rubáiyát
of
Omar Khayyám

Fifth Edition, 1889

I

WAKE! For the Sun, who scatter'd into flight
The Stars before him from the Field
   of Night,
Drives Night along with them from
   Heav'n, and strikes
The Sultán's Turret with a Shaft of
   Light.

II

BEFORE the phantom of False
   morning died,
Methought a Voice within the Tavern
   cried,
"When all the Temple is prepared
   within,
Why nods the drowsy Worshiper
   outside?"

III

AND, as the Cock crew, those who stood before
The Tavern shouted—"Open then the
    Door!
You know how little while we have
    to stay,
And, once departed, may return no
    more."

IV

NOW the New Year reviving old Desires,
The thoughtful Soul to Solitude
    retires,
Where the WHITE HAND OF MOSES
    on the Bough
Puts out, and Jesus from the Ground
    suspires.

V

IRAM indeed is gone with all his Rose,
And Jamshýd's Sev'n-ring'd Cup where no one knows;
But still a Ruby kindles in the Vine,
And many a Garden by the Water blows.

VI

AND David's lips are lockt; but in divine
High-piping Pehleví, with "Wine! Wine! Wine!
"Red Wine!"—the Nightingale cries to the Rose
That sallow cheek of hers to' incarnadine.

VII

COME, fill the Cup, and in the fire
of Spring
Your Winter garment of Repentance
  fling:
The Bird of Time has but a little way
To flutter—and the Bird is on the
  Wing.

VIII

WHETHER at Naishápúr or
Babylon,
Whether the Cup with sweet or bitter
  run,
The Wine of Life keeps oozing drop
  by drop,
The Leaves of Life keep falling one
  by one.

IX

EACH Morn a thousand Roses brings, you say:
Yes, but where leaves the Rose of
  Yesterday?
And this first Summer month that
  brings the Rose
Shall take Jamshýd and Kaikobád
  away.

X

WELL, let it take them! What have we to do
With Kaikobád the Great, or
  Kaikhosrú?
Let Zál and Rustum bluster as they
  will,
Or Hatim call to Supper—heed not
  you.

XI

WITH me along the strip of
Herbage strown
That just divides the desert from the
sown,
Where name of Slave and Sultán is
forgot—
And Peace to Mahmud on his golden
Throne!

XII

A BOOK of Verses underneath the
Bough,
A Jug of Wine, a Loaf of Bread—and
Thou
Beside me singing in the Wilderness—
Oh, Wilderness were Paradise enow!

XIII

SOME for the Glories of This
World; and some
Sigh for the Prophet's Paradise to
    come;
Ah, take the Cash, and let the Credit
    go,
Nor heed the rumble of a distant
    Drum!

XIV

LOOK to the blowing Rose about
us—"Lo,
Laughing," she says, "into the world I
    blow,
At once the silken tassel of my Purse
Tear, and its Treasure on the Garden
    throw."

XV

AND those who husbanded the Golden grain,
And those who flung it to the winds
like Rain,
Alike to no such aureate Earth are
turn'd
As, buried once, Men want dug up
again.

XVI

THE Worldly Hope men set their
Hearts upon
Turns Ashes—or it prospers; and
anon,
Like Snow upon the Desert's dusty
Face,
Lighting a little hour or two—is gone.

XVII

THINK, in this batter'd Caravanserai
  Whose Portals are alternate Night
    and Day,
How Sultán after Sultán with his
    Pomp
Abode his destined Hour, and went
    his way.

XVIII

THEY say the Lion and the Lizard
  keep
The courts where Jamshýd gloried
    and drank deep:
And Bahrám, that great Hunter—the
    Wild Ass
Stamps o'er his Head, but cannot
    break his Sleep.

XIX

I sometimes think that never blows
   so red
The Rose as where some buried
   Cæsar bled;
That every Hyacinth the Garden
   wears
Dropt in her Lap from some once
   lovely Head.

XX

AND this reviving Herb whose
   tender Green
Fledges the River-Lip on which we
   lean—
Ah, lean upon it lightly! for who
   knows
From what once lovely Lip it springs
   unseen!

XXI

AH, my Belovéd, fill the Cup that clears
To-DAY of past Regrets and future
    Fears:
To-morrow—Why, To-morrow I
    may be
Myself with Yesterday's Sev'n
    thousand Years.

XXII

FOR some we loved, the loveliest
    and the best
That from his Vintage rolling Time
    hath prest,
Have drunk their Cup a Round or
    two before,
And one by one crept silently to rest.

XXIII

AND we, that now make merry in
  the Room
They left, and Summer dresses in new
  bloom,
Ourselves must we beneath the
  Couch of Earth
Descend—ourselves to make a
  Couch—for whom?

XXIV

AH, make the most of what we yet
  may spend,
Before we too into the Dust
  descend;
Dust into Dust, and under Dust to
  lie,
Sans Wine, sans Song, sans Singer,
  and—sans End!

XXV

ALIKE for those who for To-Day prepare,
And those that after some To-Morrow stare,
   A Muezzin from the Tower of Darkness cries,
"Fools! your Reward is neither Here nor There."

XXVI

WHY, all the Saints and Sages who discuss'd
Of the Two Worlds so wisely—they are thrust
   Like foolish Prophets forth; their Words to Scorn
Are scatter'd, and their Mouths are stopt with Dust.

XXVII

MYSELF when young did eagerly frequent
Doctor and Saint, and heard great
  argument
About it and about: but evermore
Came out by the same door where in
  I went.

XXVIII

WITH them the seed of Wisdom
  did I sow,
And with mine own hand wrought to
  make it grow;
And this was all the Harvest that I
  reap'd—
"I came like Water, and like Wind I
  go."

XXIX

INTO this Universe, and Why not
knowing
Nor Whence, like Water willy-nilly
flowing;
And out of it, as Wind along the
Waste,
I know not Whither, willy-nilly
blowing.

XXX

WHAT, without asking, hither
hurried Whence?
And, without asking, Whither hurried
hence!
Oh, many a Cup of this forbidden
Wine
Must drown the memory of that
insolence!

XXXI

UP from Earth's Center through
the Seventh Gate
I rose, and on the Throne of Saturn
sate,
And many a Knot unravel'd by the
Road;
But not the Master-knot of Human
Fate.

XXXII

THERE was the Door to which I
found no Key;
There was the Veil through which I
might not see:
Some little talk awhile of ME and
THEE
There was—and then no more of
THEE and ME.

XXXIII

EARTH could not answer; nor the Seas that mourn
In flowing Purple, of their Lord
   Forlorn;
Nor rolling Heaven, with all his Signs
   reveal'd
And hidden by the sleeve of Night
   and Morn.

XXXIV

THEN of the THEE IN ME who works behind
The Veil, I lifted up my hands to
   find
A lamp amid the Darkness; and I
   heard,
As from Without—"THE ME WITHIN
   THEE BLIND!"

XXXV

THEN to the Lip of this poor earthen Urn
I lean'd, the Secret of my Life to
    learn:
And Lip to Lip it murmur'd—"While
    you live,
Drink!—for, once dead, you never
    shall return."

XXXVI

I think the Vessel, that with fugitive
Articulation answer'd, once did live,
And drink; and Ah! the passive Lip I
    kiss'd,
How many Kisses might it take—and
    give!

XXXVII

FOR I remember stopping by the
way
To watch a Potter thumping his wet
    Clay:
And with its all-obliterated Tongue
It murmur'd—"Gently, Brother,
    gently, pray!"

XXXVIII

AND has not such a Story from
of Old
Down Man's successive generations
    roll'd
Of such a clod of saturated Earth
Cast by the Maker into Human
    mold?

XXXIX

AND not a drop that from our Cups we throw
For Earth to drink of, but may steal
    below
To quench the fire of Anguish in some
    Eye
There hidden—far beneath, and long
    ago.

XL

AS then the Tulip for her morning sup
Of Heav'nly Vintage from the soil
    looks up,
Do you devoutly do the like, till
    Heav'n
To Earth invert you—like an empty
    Cup.

XLI

PERPLEXT no more with Human
or Divine,
To-morrow's tangle to the winds
resign,
And lose your fingers in the tresses
of
The Cypress-slender Minister of
Wine.

XLII

AND if the Wine you drink, the
Lip you press,
End in what All begins and ends in—
Yes;
Think then you are TO-DAY what
YESTERDAY
You were—TO-MORROW you shall
not be less.

XLIII

SO when that Angel of the darker Drink
At last shall find you by the river-
   brink,
And, offering his Cup, invite your
   Soul
Forth to your Lips to quaff—you
   shall not shrink.

XLIV

WHY, if the Soul can fling the
   Dust aside,
And naked on the Air of Heaven
   ride,
Were't not a Shame—were't not a
   Shame for him
In this clay carcass crippled to abide?

XLV

'TIS but a Tent where takes his one
    day's rest
A Sultán to the realm of Death
    addrest;
The Sultán rises, and the dark
    Ferrásh
Strikes, and prepares it for another
    Guest.

XLVI

AND fear not lest Existence
    closing your
Account, and mine, should know the
    like no more;
The Eternal Saki from that Bowl has
    pour'd
Millions of Bubbles like us, and will
    pour.

XLVII

WHEN You and I behind the Veil
  are past,
Oh, but the long, long while the
  World shall last,
Which of our Coming and Departure
  heeds
As the Sea's self should heed a
  pebble-cast.

XLVIII

A Moment's Halt—a momentary
  taste
Of BEING from the Well amid the
  Waste—
And Lo!—the phantom Caravan has
  reach'd
The NOTHING it set out from—Oh,
  make haste!

XLIX

WOULD you that spangle of
    Existence spend
About THE SECRET—quick about it,
    Friend!
A Hair perhaps divides the False from
    True—
And upon what, prithee, may life
    depend?

L

A Hair perhaps divides the False
    and True;
Yes; and a single Alif were the clue—
Could you but find it—to the
    Treasure-house,
And peradventure to THE MASTER
    too;

LI

WHOSE secret Presence through
Creation's veins
Running Quicksilver-like eludes your
pains;
Taking all shapes from Máh to
Máhi and
They change and perish all—but HE
remains;

LII

A moment guessed—then back
behind the Fold
Immerst of Darkness round the
Drama roll'd
Which, for the Pastime of Eternity,
He doth Himself contrive, enact,
behold.

LIII

BUT if in vain, down on the
 stubborn floor
Of Earth, and up to Heav'n's
 unopening Door,
You gaze TO-DAY, while You are
 You—how then
TO-MORROW, when You shall be You
 no more?

LIV

WASTE not your Hour, nor in
 the vain pursuit
Of This and That endeavor and
 dispute;
Better be jocund with the fruitful
 Grape
Than sadden after none, or bitter,
 Fruit.

LV

YOU know, my Friends, with what
a brave Carouse
I made a Second Marriage in my
house;
Divorced old barren Reason from my
Bed,
And took the Daughter of the Vine to
Spouse.

LVI

FOR "Is" and "Is-NOT" though
with Rule and Line
And "UP-AND-DOWN" by Logic I
define,
Of all that one should care to
fathom, I
was never deep in anything but—
Wine.

LVII

AH, by my Computations, People say,
Reduce the Year to better
   reckoning?—Nay,
'Twas only striking from the
   Calendar
Unborn To-morrow and dead
   Yesterday.

LVIII

AND lately, by the Tavern Door agape,
Came shining through the Dusk an
   Angel Shape
Bearing a Vessel on his Shoulder; and
He bid me taste of it; and 'twas—the
   Grape!

LIX

THE Grape that can with Logic
    absolute
The Two-and-Seventy jarring Sects
    confute:
The sovereign Alchemist that in a
    trice
Life's leaden metal into Gold
    transmute;

LX

THE mighty Mahmud, Allah-
    breathing Lord,
That all the misbelieving and black
    Horde
Of Fears and Sorrows that infest the
    Soul
Scatters before him with his
    whirlwind Sword.

LXI

WHY, be this Juice the growth of
    God, who dare
Blaspheme the twisted tendril as a
    Snare?
A Blessing, we should use it, should
    we not?
And if a Curse—why, then, Who set it
    there?

LXII

I must abjure the Balm of Life, I
    must,
Scared by some After-reckoning ta'en
    on trust,
Or lured with Hope of some Diviner
    Drink,
To fill the Cup—when crumbled into
    Dust!

LXIII

OH threats of Hell and Hopes of
  Paradise!
One thing at least is certain—*This*
  Life flies;
One thing is certain and the rest is
  Lies;
The Flower that once has blown for
  ever dies.

LXIV

STRANGE, is it not? that of the
  myriads who
Before us pass'd the door of Darkness
  through,
Not one returns to tell us of the
  Road,
Which to discover we must travel
  too.

LXV

THE Revelations of Devout and Learn'd
Who rose before us, and as Prophets burn'd,
Are all but Stories, which, awoke from Sleep
They told their comrades, and to Sleep return'd.

LXVI

I sent my Soul through the Invisible,
Some letter of that After-life to spell:
And by and by my Soul return'd to me,
And answer'd "I Myself am Heav'n and Hell:"

LXVII

HEAV'N but the Vision of fulfill'd
  Desire,
And Hell the Shadow from a Soul on
  fire,
Cast on the Darkness into which
  Ourselves,
So late emerged from, shall so soon
  expire.

LXVIII

WE are no other than a moving
  row
Of Magic Shadow-shapes that come
  and go
Round with the Sun-illumined
  Lantern held
In Midnight by the Master of the
  Show;

LXIX

BUT helpless Pieces of the Game
He plays
Upon this Chequer-board of Nights
and Days;
Hither and thither moves, and checks,
and slays,
And one by one back in the Closet
lays.

LXX

THE Ball no question makes of
Ayes and Noes,
But Here or There as strikes the
Player goes;
And He that toss'd you down into
the Field,
He knows about it all—HE knows—
HE knows!

LXXI

THE Moving Finger writes; and,
having writ,
Moves on: nor all your Piety nor
Wit
Shall lure it back to cancel half a
Line,
Nor all your Tears wash out a Word
of it.

LXXII

AND that inverted Bowl they call
the Sky,
Whereunder crawling coop'd we live
and die,
Lift not your hands to It for help—
for It
As impotently moves as you or I.

LXXIII

WITH Earth's first Clay They did the Last Man knead,
And there of the Last Harvest sow'd the Seed:
And the first Morning of Creation wrote
What the Last Dawn of Reckoning shall read.

LXXIV

YESTERDAY This Day's Madness did prepare;
To-Morrow's Silence, Triumph, or Despair:
Drink! for you not know whence you came, nor why:
Drink! for you know not why you go, nor where.

LXXV

I tell you this—When, started from
the Goal,
Over the flaming shoulders of the
Foal
Of Heav'n Parwín and Mushtari they
flung,
In my predestined Plot of Dust and
Soul.

LXXVI

THE Vine had struck a fiber: which about
It clings my Being—let the Dervish
flout;
Of my Base metal may be filed a Key
That shall unlock the Door he howls
without.

LXXVII

AND this I know: whether the one True Light
Kindle to Love, or Wrath consume me quite,
One Flash of It within the Tavern caught
Better than in the Temple lost outright.

LXXVIII

WHAT! out of senseless Nothing to provoke
A conscious Something to resent the yoke
Of unpermitted Pleasure, under pain
Of Everlasting Penalties, if broke!

LXXIX

WHAT! from his helpless
  Creature be repaid
Pure Gold for what he lent him dross-
    allay'd—
Sue for a Debt he never did contract,
And cannot answer—Oh the sorry
    trade!

LXXX

OH Thou, who didst with pitfall
  and with gin
Beset the Road I was to wander in,
Thou wilt not with Predestined Evil
    round
Enmesh, and then impute my Fall to
    Sin!

LXXXI

OH Thou, who Man of baser
Earth didst make,
And ev'n with Paradise devise the
Snake:
For all the Sin wherewith the Face of
Man
Is blacken'd—Man's forgiveness
give—and take!

LXXXII

AS under cover of departing Day
Slunk hunger-stricken Ramazan
away,
Once more within the Potter's house
alone
I stood, surrounded by the Shapes of
Clay.

LXXXIII

SHAPES of all Sorts and Sizes, great
and small,
That stood along the floor and by the
    wall;
And some loquacious Vessels were;
    and some
Listen'd perhaps, but never talk'd at
    all.

LXXXIV

SAID one among them—"Surely
not in vain
My substance of the common Earth
    was ta'en
And to this Figure molded, to be
    broke,
Or trampled back to shapeless Earth
    again."

LXXXV

THEN said a Second—"Ne'er a peevish Boy
Would break the Bowl from which he
    drank in joy;
And He that with his hand the Vessel
    made
Will surely not in after Wrath
    destroy."

LXXXVI

AFTER a momentary silence spake
Some Vessel of a more ungainly
    Make;
"They sneer at me for leaning all
    awry:
What! did the Hand then of the
    Potter shake?"

LXXXVII

WHEREAT some one of the
    loquacious Lot—
I think a Súfi pipkin—waxing hot—
"All this of Pot and Potter—Tell me
    then,
Who is the Potter, pray, and who the
    Pot?"

LXXXVIII

"WHY," said another, "Some
    there are who tell
Of one who threatens he will toss to
    Hell
The luckless Pots he marr'd in
    making—Pish!
He's a Good Fellow, and 'twill all be
    well."

LXXXIX

"WELL," murmured one, "Let
        whoso make or buy,
My Clay with long Oblivion is gone
        dry:
But fill me with the old familiar
        Juice,
Methinks I might recover by and
        by."

XC

SO while the Vessels one by one
        were speaking,
The little Moon look'd in that all
        were seeking:
And then they jogg'd each other,
        "Brother! Brother!
Now for the Porter's shoulders' knot
        a-creaking!"

XCI

AH, with the Grape my fading life
provide,
And wash the Body whence the Life
has died,
And lay me, shrouded in the living
Leaf,
By some not unfrequented Garden-
side.

XCII

THAT ev'n buried Ashes such a
snare
Of Vintage shall fling up into the
Air
As not a True-believer passing by
But shall be overtaken unaware.

XCIII

INDEED the Idols I have loved so
    long
Have done my credit in this World
    much wrong:
Have drown'd my Glory in a shallow
    Cup,
And sold my reputation for a Song.

XCIV

INDEED, indeed, Repentance oft
    before
I swore—but was I sober when I
    swore?
And then and then came Spring, and
    Rose-in-hand
My thread-bare Penitence apieces
    tore.

XCV

AND much as Wine has play'd the
Infidel,
And robb'd me of my Robe of
Honor—Well,
I wonder often what the Vintners
buy
One half so precious as the stuff
they sell.

XCVI

YET Ah, that Spring should vanish
with the Rose!
That Youth's sweet-scented
manuscript should close!
The Nightingale that in the branches
sang,
Ah whence, and whither flown again,
who knows!

XCVII

WOULD but the Desert of the Fountain yield
One glimpse—if dimly, yet indeed, reveal'd,
To which the fainting Traveler might spring,
As springs the trampled herbage of the field!

XCVIII

WOULD but some wingéd Angel ere too late
Arrest the yet unfolded Roll of Fate,
And make the stern Recorder otherwise
Enregister, or quite obliterate!

XCIX

AH Love! could you and I with Him conspire
To grasp this sorry Scheme of Things entire,
  Would not we shatter it to bits—and then
Re-mold it nearer to the Heart's Desire!

C

YON rising Moon that looks for us again—
How oft hereafter will she wax and wane;
  How oft hereafter rising look for us
Through this same Garden—and for one in vain!

CI

AND when like her, oh Saki, you shall pass
Among the Guests Star-scatter'd on
  the Grass,
And in your joyous errand reach the
  spot
Where I made One—turn down an
  empty Glass!

TAMÁM.

NOTES

The references are, except in the first note only, to the Quatrains of the Fifth edition.

QUATRAIN I

Flinging a Stone into the Cup was the signal for "To Horse!" in the Desert.

II

The "False Dawn"; *Subhi Kázib*, a transient Light on the Horizon about an hour before the *Subhi sádik* or True Dawn; a well-known Phenomenon in the East.

IV

New Year. Beginning with the Vernal Equinox, it must be remembered; and (howsoever the old Solar Year is practically superseded by the clumsy *Lunar* Year that dates from the Mohammedan Hijra) still commemorated by a Festival that is said to have been appointed by the very Jamshýd whom Omar so often talks of, and whose yearly Calendar he helped to rectify.

"The sudden approach and rapid advance of the Spring," says Mr. Binning, [*Two Years' Travel in Persia &c 1.165*] "are very striking. Before the Snow is well off the Ground, the Trees burst into Blossom, and the Flowers start from the Soil. At *Naw Rooz* (*their* New Year's Day) the Snow was lying in patches on the Hills and in the shaded Vallies, while the Fruit-trees in the Garden were budding beautifully, and green Plants and Flowers springing upon the Plains on every side—

> *And on old Hyems' Chin and icy Crown*
> *An odorous Chaplet of sweet Summer buds*
> *Is, as in mockery, set—*

Among the Plants newly appear'd I recognized some Acquaintances I had not seen for many a Year: among these, two varieties of the Thistle; coarse species of the Daisy, like the Horse-gowan; red and white clover; the Dock; the blue Cornflower; and that vulgar Herb the Dandelion rearing its yellow crest on the Banks of the Water-courses." The Nightingale was not yet heard, for the Rose was not yet blown: but an almost identical Blackbird and Woodpecker helped to make up something of a North-country Spring.

"The White Hand of Moses." Exodus iv. 6; where Moses draws forth his Hand—not, according to the Persians, "*leprous as Snow*," but *white*, as our May-blossom in Spring perhaps. According to them also the Healing Power of Jesus resided in his Breath.

V

Iram, planted by King Shaddád, and now sunk somewhere in the Sands of Arabia. Jamshýd's Seven-ring'd Cup was typical of the 7 Heavens, 7 Planets, 7 Seas, &c., and was a *Divining Cup*.

VI

Pehleví, the old Heroic *Sanskrit* of Persia. Háfiz also speaks of the Nightingale's *Pehleví*, which did not change with the People's.

I am not sure if the fourth line refers to the Red Rose looking sickly, or to the Yellow Rose that ought to be Red; Red, White and Yellow Roses all common in Persia. I think that Southey in his Common-Place Book, quotes from some Spanish author about the Rose being White till 10 o'clock; "Rosa Perfecta" at 2; and "perfecta incarnada" at 5.

X

Rustum, the "Hercules" of Persia, and Zal his Father, whose exploits are among the most celebrated in the Shahnama. Hatim Tai, a well-known type of Oriental Generosity.

XIII

A Drum—beaten outside a Palace.

XIV

That is, the Rose's Golden Centre.

XVIII

Persepolis: call'd also *Takht-i-Jam-shyd*—THE THRONE OF JAMSHÝD, "*King Splendid*," of the mythical *Peshdádian* Dynasty, and supposed (according to the Shah-nama) to have been founded and built by him.

Others refer it to the Work of the Genie King, Ján Ibn Ján—who also built the Pyramids—before the time of Adam.

BAHRÁM GUR.—*Bahram of the Wild Ass*—a Sassanian Sovereign—had also his Seven Castles (like the King of Bohemia!) each of a different Colour: each with a Royal Mistress within; each of whom tells him a Story, as told in one of the most famous Poems of Persia, written by Amir Khusraw: all these Sevens also figuring (according to Eastern Mysticism) the Seven Heavens; and perhaps the Book itself that Eighth, into which the mystical Seven transcend, and within which they revolve. The Ruins of Three of those Towers are yet shown by the Peasantry; as also the Swamp in which Bahram sunk, like the Master of Ravenswood, while pursuing his Gúr.

> *The Palace that to Heav'n his pillars threw,*
> *And Kings the forehead on his threshold drew—*
> *I saw the solitary Ringdove there,*
> *And "Coo, coo, coo," she cried; and "Coo, coo, coo."*

This Quatrain Mr. Binning found, among several of Háfiz and others, inscribed by some stray hand among the ruins of Persepolis. The Ringdove's ancient *Pehleví Coo, Coo, Coo*, signifies also in Persian "*Where? Where? Where?*" In Attar's "Bird-parliament" she is reproved by the Leader of the Birds for sitting still, and for ever harping on that one note of lamentation for her lost Yúsuf. Apropos of Omar's Red Roses in Quatrain XIX, I am reminded of an old English Superstition, that our Anemone Pulsatilla, or purple "Pasque Flower," (which grows plentifully about the Fleam Dyke, near Cambridge,) grows only where Danish Blood has been spilt.

XXI

A thousand years to each Planet.

XXXI

Saturn, Lord of the Seventh Heaven.

XXXII

Me-And-Thee: some dividual Existence or Personality distinct from the Whole.

XXXVII

One of the Persian Poets—Attar, I think—has a pretty story about this. A thirsty Traveller dips his hand into a Spring of Water to drink from. By-and-by comes another who draws up and drinks from an earthen bowl, and then departs, leaving his Bowl behind him. The first Traveller takes it up for another draught; but is surprised to find that the same Water which had tasted sweet from his own hand tastes bitter from the earthen Bowl. But a Voice—from Heaven, I think—tells him the clay from which the Bowl is made was once *Man*; and, into whatever shape renew'd, can never lose the bitter flavour of Mortality.

XXXIX

The custom of throwing a little Wine on the ground before drinking still continues in Persia, and perhaps generally in the East. Mons. Nicolas considers it "un signe de libéralité, et en même temps un avertissement que le buveur doit vider sa coupe jusqu'à la dernière goutte." Is it not more likely an ancient Superstition; a Libation to propitiate Earth, or make her an Accomplice in the illicit Revel? Or, perhaps, to divert the Jealous Eye by some sacrifice of superfluity, as with the Ancients of the West? With Omar we see something more is signified; the precious Liquor is not lost, but sinks into the ground to refresh the dust of some poor Wine-worshipper foregone.

Thus Háfiz, copying Omar in so many ways: "When thou drinkest Wine pour a draught on the ground. Wherefore fear the Sin which brings to another Gain?"

XLIII

According to one beautiful Oriental Legend, Azräel accomplishes his mission by holding to the nostril an Apple from the Tree of Life.

This, and the two following Stanzas would have been withdrawn, as somewhat *de trop*, from the Text, but for advice which I least like to disregard.

LI

From Máh to Máhi; from Fish to Moon.

LVI

A Jest, of course, at his Studies. A curious mathe-matical Quatrain of Omar's has been pointed out to me; the more curious because almost exactly parallel'd by some Verses of Doctor Donne's, that are quoted in Izaak Walton's Lives! Here is Omar: "You and I are the image of a pair of compasses; though we have two heads (SC. our *feet*) we have one body; when we have fixed the centre for our circle, we bring our heads (SC. feet) together at the end." Dr. Donne:

If we be two, we two are so
As stiff twin-compasses are two;
Thy Soul, the fixt foot, makes no show
To move, but does if the other do.

And though thine in the centre sit,
Yet when my other far does roam,
Thine leans and hearkens after it,
And rows erect as mine comes home.

Such thou must be to me, who must
Like the other foot obliquely run;
Thy firmness makes my circle just,
And me to end where I begun.

LIX

The Seventy-two Religions supposed to divide the World, *including* Islamism, as some think: but others not.

LX

Alluding to Sultán Mahmud's Conquest of India and its dark people.

LXVIII

Fanusi khiyal, a Magic-lantern still used in India; the cylindrical Interior being painted with various Figures, and so lightly poised and ventilated as to revolve round the lighted Candle within.

LXX

A very mysterious Line in the Original:

   O danad O danad O danad O—

breaking off something like our Wood-pigeon's Note, which she is said to take up just where she left off.

LXXV

Parwín and Mushtari—The Pleiads and Jupiter.

LXXXVII

This Relation of Pot and Potter to Man and his Maker figures far and wide in the Literature of the World, from the time of the Hebrew Prophets to the present; when it may finally take the name of "Pot theism," by which Mr. Carlyle ridiculed Sterling's "Pantheism." *My* Sheikh, whose knowledge flows in from all quarters, writes to me—

"Apropos of old Omar's Pots, did I ever tell you the sentence I found in 'Bishop Pearson on the Creed'? 'Thus are we wholly at the disposal of His will, and our present and future condition framed and ordered by His free, but wise and just, decrees. *Hath not the potter power over the clay, of the same lump to make one vessel unto honour, and another unto dishonour?* (Rom. ix. 21.) And can that earth-artificer have a freer power over his *brother potsherd* (both being made of the same metal), than God hath over him, who, by the strange fecundity of His omnipotent power, first made the clay out of nothing, and then him out of that?'" And again— from a very different quarter—"I had to refer the other day to Aristophanes, and came by chance on a curious Speaking-pot story in the Vespæ [*The Wasps*, lines 1435–40),—

Φιλοκλέων
ἄκουε, μὴ φεῦγ᾽. ἐν Συβάρει γυνή ποτε
κατέαξ ἐχῖνον.

Κατήγορος
ταῦτ ἐγὼ μαρτύρομαι.

Φιλοκλέων
οὐχῖνος οὖν ἔχων τιν᾽ ἐπεμαρτύρατο·
εἶθ ἡ Συβαρῖτις εἶπεν, ʽεἰ ναὶ τὰν κόραν
τὴν μαρτυριαν ταύτην ἐάσας ἐν τάχει
ἐπίδεσμον ἐπρίω, νοῦν ἂν εἶχες πλείονα.᾽

PHILOCLEON:
   Listen, instead of going off so abruptly. A woman at Sybaris broke a box.

ACCUSER, *to his witness*:
   I again ask you to witness this.

PHILOCLEON:
   The box therefore had the fact attested, but the woman said, "Never worry about witnessing the matter, but hurry off to buy a cord to tie it together with; that will be the more sensible course."

which I had quite forgotten.

"The Pot calls a bystander to be a witness to his bad treatment. The woman says, 'If, by Proserpine, instead of all this 'testifying' (comp. Cuddie and his mother in 'Old Mortality!') you would buy yourself a rivet, it would show more sense in you!' The Scholiast explains *echinus* as any bowl from the potter." One more illustration for the oddity's sake from the "Autobiography of a Cornish Rector," by the late James Hamley Tregenna, 1871.

"There was one odd Fellow in our Company—he was so like a Figure in the 'Pilgrim's Progress' that Richard always called him the 'ALLEGORY,' with a long white beard—a rare Appendage in those days—and a Face the colour of which seemed to have been baked in, like the Faces one used to see on Earthenware Jugs. In our Country-dialect Earthenware is called '*Clome*'; so the Boys of the Village used to shout out after him—'Go back to the Potter, Old Clome-face, and get baked over again.' For the 'Allegory,' though shrewd enough in most things, had the reputation of being '*saift-baked*,' i.e., of weak intellect."

XC

At the Close of the Fasting Month, Ramazan (which makes the Mussulman unhealthy and unamiable), the first Glimpse of the New Moon (who rules their division of the Year) is looked for with the utmost Anxiety, and hailed with Acclamation. Then it is that the Porter's Knot maybe heard—toward the *Cellar*. Omar has elsewhere a pretty Quatrain about the same Moon—

"Be of Good Cheer—the sullen Month will die,
And a young Moon requite us by and by:
Look how the Old one meagre, bent, and wan
With Age and Fast, is fainting from the Sky!"

THE LIFE
of
JÁMÍ

EDWARD FITZGERALD
London 1904

Notice of Jámí's Life

[I hope the following disproportionate Notice of Jámí's Life will be amusing enough to excuse its length. I found most of it at the last moment in Rosenzweig's "Biographische Notizen" of Jámí, from whose own, and Commentator's, Works it purports to be gathered. – E.F.]

Núruddín Abdurrahman, Son of Maulána Nizamuddin[1] Ahmed, and descended on the Mother's side from One of the Four great "Fathers" of Islamism, was born AH 817, AD 1414, in Jám, a little Town of Khorásan, whither (according to the Heft Aklím—"Seven Climates") his Grandfather had migrated from Desht of Ispahán, and from which the Poet ultimately took his Takhalus, or Poetic name, Jámí. This word also signifies "A Cup;" wherefore, he says, "Born in Jám, and dipt in the "*Jam*" of Holy Lore, for a double reason I must be called Jámí in the Book of Song." He was celebrated afterwards in other Oriental Titles— "Lord of Poets"—"Elephant of Wisdom", &c., but often liked to call himself "The Ancient of Herát", where he mainly resided.

---

1 Such final "uddins" signify "Of the Faith." "Maulána" may be taken as "Master" in Learning, Law, etc.

When Five Years old he received the name of Núruddín—the "Light of Faith", and even so early began to show the Metal, and take the Stamp that distinguished him through Life. In 1419, a famous Sheikh, Khwájah Mehmed Parsa, then in the last year of his Life, was being carried through Jám. "I was not then Five Years old", says Jámí, "and my Father, who with his Friends went forth to salute him, had me carried on the Shoulders of one of the Family and set down before the Litter of the Sheikh, who gave a Nosegay into my hand. Sixty years have passed, and methinks I now see before me the bright Image of the Holy Man, and feel the Blessing of his Aspect, from which I date my after Devotion to that Brotherhood in which I hope to be enrolled."

So again, when Maulána Fakhruddín Loristani had alighted at his Mother's house—"I was then so little that he set me upon his Knee, and with his Fingers drawing the Letters of 'Alí' and 'Omar' in the Air, laughed delightedly to hear me spell them. He also by his Goodness sowed in my Heart the Seed of his Devotion, which has grown to Increase within me—in which I hope to live, and in which to die. Oh God! Dervish let me live, and Dervish die; and in the Company of the Dervish do Thou quicken me to Life again!"

Jámí first went to a School at Herát; and afterward to one founded by the Great Timúr at Samarcand.

There he not only outstript his Fellows in the very Encyclopaedic Studies of Persian Education, but even puzzled the Doctors in Logic, Astronomy, and Theology; who, however, with unresenting Gravity welcomed him—

"Lo! a new Light added to our Galaxy!"

—In the wider Field of Samarcand he might have liked to remain; but Destiny liked otherwise, and a Dream recalled him to Herát. A Vision of the Great Súfi Master there, Mehmed Saaduddín Kaschgari, of the Nakhsbend Order of Dervishes, appeared to him in his Sleep, and bade him return to One who would satisfy all Desire. Jámí went back to Herát; he saw the Sheikh discoursing with his Disciples by the Door of the Great Mosque; day after day passed by without daring to present himself; but the Master's Eye was upon him; day by day draws him nearer and nearer—till at last the Sheikh announces to those about him—

"Lo! this Day have I taken a Falcon in my Snare!"

Under him Jámí began his Súfi Noviciate, with such Devotion, and under such Fascination from the Master, that going, he tells us, but for one Summer

Day's Holiday into the Country, one single Line was enough to "lure the Tassel-gentle back again;"

"Lo! here am I, and Thou look'st on the Rose!"

By-and-bye he withdraws, by course of Súfi Instruction, into Solitude so long and profound, that on his Return to Men he has almost lost the Power of Converse with them. At last, when duly taught, and duly authorized to teach as Súfi Doctor, he yet will not, though solicited by those who had seen such a Vision of Him as had drawn Himself to Herát; and not till the Evening of his Life is he to be seen with White hairs taking that place by the Mosque which his departed Master had been used to occupy before.

Meanwhile he had become Poet, which no doubt winged his Reputation and Doctrine far and wide through a People so susceptible to poetic impulse.

"A Thousand times", he says, "I have repented of such Employment; but I could no more shirk it than one can shirk what the Pen of Fate has written on his Forehead"—"As Poet I have resounded through the World; Heaven filled itself with my Song, and the Bride of Time adorned her Ears and Neck with the Pearls of my Verse, whose coming Caravan the Persian Háfiz and Saadi came forth gladly to salute, and the Indian Khosrú and Hasan hailed as a Wonder of the World." "The Kings of India and Rúm greet me by Letter: the Lords of Irák and Tabríz load me with Gifts; and what shall I say of those of Khorasán, who drown me in an Ocean of Munificence?"

This, though Oriental, is scarcely Bombast. Jámí was honoured by Princes at home and abroad, and at the very time they were cutting one another's Throats; by his own Sultan Abou Saïd; by Hasan Beg of Mesopotamia—"Lord of Tabríz"—by whom Abou Saïd was defeated, dethroned, and slain; by Mahomet II. of Turkey—"King of Rúm"—who in his turn defeated Hasan; and lastly by Husein Mirza Baikara, who extinguished the Prince whom Hasan had set up in Abou's Place at Herát. Such is the House that Jack builds in Persia.

As Hasan Beg, however—the USUNCASSAN of old European Annals—is singularly connected with the present Poem, and with probably the most important event in Jámí's Life, I will briefly follow the Steps that led to that as well as other Princely Intercourse.

In AH 877, AD 1472, Jámí set off on his Pilgrimage to Mecca. He, and, on his Account, the Caravan he went with, were honourably and safely escorted through the intervening Countries by order of their several Potentates as far as Bagdad. There Jámí fell into trouble by the Treachery of a Follower he had reproved, and who (born 400 Years too soon) misquoted Jámí's Verse into disparagement of ALÍ, the Darling Imám of Persia. This getting wind at Bagdad, the thing was brought to solemn Tribunal, at which Hasan Beg's two Sons assisted. Jámí came victoriously off; his Accuser pilloried with a dockt Beard in Bagdad Marketplace: but the Poet was so ill pleased with the stupidity of those who believed the Report, that, standing in Verse upon the Tigris' side, he calls for a Cup of Wine to seal up Lips of whose Utterance the Men of Bagdad were unworthy.

After 4 months' stay there, during which he visits at Helleh the Tomb of Alí's Son, Husein, who had fallen at Kerbela, he sets forth again—to Najaf, where he says his Camel sprang forward at sight of Ali's own Tomb—crosses the Desert in 22 days, meditating on the Prophet's Glory, to Medina; and so at last to MECCA, where, as he sang in a Ghazal, he went through all Mahommedan Ceremony with a Mystical Understanding of his Own.

He then turns Homeward: is entertained for 45 days at Damascus, which he leaves the very Day before the Turkish Mahomet's Envoys come with 5000 Ducats to carry him to Constantinople. Arriving at Amida, the Capital of Mesopotamia (Diyak bakar), he finds War broken out in full Flame between that Mahomet and Hasan Beg, King of the Country, who has Jámí honourably escorted through the dangerous Roads to Tabríz; there receives him in Díván, and would fain have him abide at Court awhile. Jámí, however, is intent on Home, and once more seeing his aged Mother—for *he* is turned of Sixty!—and at last touches Herát in the Month of Schaaban, 1473, after the Average Year's absence.

This is the HASAN, "in Name and Nature *Handsome*" (and so described by some Venetian Ambassadors of the Time), of whose protection Jámí speaks in the Preliminary Vision of this Poem, which he dedicates to Hasan's Son, Yacúb Beg: who, after the due murder of an Elder Brother, succeeded to the Throne; till all the Dynasties of "Black and White Sheep" together were swept away a few years after by Ismael, Founder of the Sofí Dynasty in Persia.

Arrived at home, Jámí finds Husein Mirzá Baikará, last of the Timúridae, fast seated there; having probably slain ere Jámí went the Prince whom Hasan had set up; but the date of a Year or Two may well wander in the Bloody Jungle of Persian History. Husein, however, receives Jámí with open Arms; Nisámuddín Alí Schír, his Vizir, a Poet too, had hailed in Verse the Poet's Advent from Damascus as "The Moon rising in the West;" and they both continued affectionately to honour him as long as he lived.

Jámí sickened of his mortal Illness on the 13th of Moharrem, 1492—a Sunday. His Pulse began to fail on the following Friday, about the Hour of Morning Prayer, and stopped at the very moment when the Muezzin began to call to Evening. He had lived Eighty-one years. Sultan Husein undertook the Burial of one whose Glory it was to have lived and died in Dervish Poverty; the Dignities of the Kingdom followed him to the Grave; where 20 days afterward was recited in presence of the Sultan and his Court an Eulogy composed by the Vizír, who also laid the first Stone of a Monument to his Friend's Memory—the first Stone of "Tarbet 'i Jámí", in the Street of Mesched, a principal Thoro'fare of the City of Herát. For, says Rosenzweig, it must be kept in mind that Jámí was reverenced not only as a Poet and Philosopher, but as a Saint also; who not only might work a Miracle himself, but leave the Power lingering about his Tomb. It was known that once in his Life, an Arab, who had falsely accused him of selling a Camel he knew to be mortally unsound, had very shortly after died, as Jámí had predicted, and on the very selfsame spot where the Camel fell. And that Libellous Rogue at Baghdád—he, putting his hand into his Horse's Nose-bag to see if "das Thier" has finisht his Corn, had his Forefinger bitten off by the same—"von demselben der Zeigefinger abgebissen"—of which "Verstümmlung" he soon died—I suppose, as he ought, of Lock jaw.

The Persians, who are adepts at much elegant Ingenuity, are fond of commemorating Events by some analogous Word or Sentence whose Letters, cabalistically corresponding to certain Numbers, compose the Date required. In Jámí's case they have hit upon the word "Kus", A Cup, whose signification brings his own name to Memory, and whose relative Letters make up his 81 years. They have *Taríks* also for remembering the Year of his Death: Rosenzweig gives some; but Ouseley the prettiest, if it will hold:—

Dúd az Khorásán bar ámed—
"The smoke" of Sighs "went up from Khorásán."

No Biographer, says Rosenzweig cautiously, records of Jámí that he had more than one Wife (Granddaughter of his Master Sheikh) and Four Sons; which, however, are Five too many for the Doctrine of this Poem. Of the Sons, Three died Infant; and the Fourth (born to him in very old Age), and for whom he wrote some Elementary Tracts, and the more famous "Beharistan" lived but a few years, and was remembered by his Father in the Preface to his Chiradnámeh Iskander—a book of Morals— which perhaps had also been begun for the Boy's Instruction.

Of Jámí's wonderful Fruitfulness—"bewunderungs- werther Fruchtbarkeit"—as Writer, Rosenzweig names Forty-four offsprings—the Letters of the word "Jám" completing by the aforesaid process that very Number. But Shár Khán Lúdi in his

"Memoirs of the Poets", says Ouseley, counts him Author of *Ninety-nine* Volumes of Grammar, Poetry, and Theology, which "continue to be universally admired in all parts of the Eastern World, Irán, Turán, and Hindústán"—copied some of them into precious Manuscript, illuminated with Gold and Painting, by the greatest Penmen and Artists of the Time; one such—the "Beháristán"—said to have cost Thousands of Pounds—autographed as one most precious treasure of their Libraries by two Sovereign Descendants of TIMÚR upon the Throne of Hindústán; and now reposited away from "the Drums and Tramplings" of Oriental Conquest in the tranquil Seclusion of an English Library.

Of these Ninety-nine, or Forty-four Volumes few are known, and none except the Present and one other Poem ever printed, in England, where the knowledge of Persian might have been politically useful. The Poet's name with us is almost solely associated with "Yúsuf and Zulaikhá", which, with the other two I have mentioned, count Three of the Brother Stars of that Constellation into which Jámí, or his Admirers, have clustered his Seven best Mystical Poems under the name of "HEFT AURANG"—those "SEVEN THRONES" to which we of the West and North give our characteristic Name of "Great Bear" and "Charles's Wain."

He must have enjoyed great Favour and Protection from his Princes at home, or he would hardly have ventured to write so freely as in this Poem he does of Doctrine which exposed the Súfí to vulgar abhorrence and Danger. Háfiz and others are apologized for as having been obliged to veil a Divinity beyond what "THE PROPHET" dreamt of under the Figure of Mortal Cup and Cup-bearer. Jámí speaks in Allegory too, by way of making a palpable grasp at the Skirt of the Ineffable; but he also dares, in the very thick of Mahommedanism, to talk of Reason as sole Fountain of Prophecy; and to pant for what would seem so Pantheistic an Identification with the Deity as shall blind him to any distinction between Good and Evil.[2]

I must not forget one pretty passage of Jámí's Life. He had a nephew, one Maulána Abdullah, who was ambitious of following his Uncle's Footsteps in Poetry. Jámí first dissuaded him; then, by way of trial whether he had a Talent as well as a Taste, bid him imitate Firdúsi's Satire on Shah Mahmúd. The Nephew did so well, that Jámí then encouraged him to proceed; himself wrote the first Couplet of his First (and most noted) Poem—Laila & Majnún.

---

2 "Je me souviens d'un Prédicateur à Ispahan qui, prêchant un jour dans une Place publique, parla furieusement contre ces Soufys, disant qu'ils étoient des Athées à bruler; qu'il s'étonnoit qu'on les laissât vivre; et que de tuer un Soufy étoit une Action plus agréable à Dieu que de conserver la Vie à dix Hommes de Bien. Cinq ou Six Soufys qui étoient parmi les Auditeurs se jettèrent sur lui après le Sermon et le battirent terriblement; et comme je m'efforçois de les empêcher ils me disoient—'Un homme qui prêche le Meurtre doit-il se plaindre d'être battu?'"—CHARDIN.

This Book of which the Pen has now laid the
    Foundation,
May the diploma of Acceptance one day befall
    it,—

and Abdullah went on to write that and four other
Poems which Persia continues and multiplies in fine
Manuscript and Illumination to the present day,
remembering their Author under his Takhalus of
Hátifí—"The Voice from Heaven"—and Last of
the so reputed Persian Poets.

SALÁMÁN

&

ABSÁL

EDWARD FITZGERALD

London 1904

Preface

AN ALLEGORY

Translated from the Persian of Jámi by
Edward Fitzgerald London 1904

My dear Cowell,

Two years ago, when we began (I for the first time) to read this Poem together, I wanted you to translate it, as something that should interest a few who are worth interesting. You, however, did not see the way clear then, and had Aristotle pulling you by one Shoulder and Prakrit Vararuchi by the other, so as indeed to have hindered you up to this time completing a Version of Háfiz' best Odes which you had then happily begun. So, continuing to like old Jámi more and more, I must try my hand upon him; and here is my reduced Version of a small Original. What Scholarship it has is yours, my Master in Persian and so much beside; who are no further answerable for *all* than by well liking and wishing publisht what you may scarce have Leisure to find due fault with.

Had all the Poem been like Parts, it would have been all translated, and in such Prose lines as you measure Háfiz in, and such as any one should adopt who does not feel himself so much of a Poet as him he translates and some he translates for—before whom it is best to lay the raw material as genuine as may be, to work up to their own better Fancies. But, unlike Háfiz' best—(whose Sonnets are sometimes as close packt as Shakespeare's, which they resemble in more ways than one)—Jámi, you know, like his Countrymen generally, is very diffuse in what he tells and his way of telling it. The very structure of the Persian Couplet—(here, like people on the Stage, I am repeating to you what you know, with an Eye to the small Audience beyond)—so often ending with the same Word, or Two Words, if but the foregoing Syllable secure a lawful Rhyme, so often makes the Second Line but a slightly varied Repetition, or Modification of the First, and gets slowly over Ground often hardly worth gaining. This iteration is common indeed to the Hebrew Psalms and Proverbs—where, however, the Value of the Repetition is different. In your Háfiz also, not Two only, but Eight or Ten Lines perhaps are tied to the same Close of Two—or *Three*—words; a verbal Ingenuity as much valued in the East as better Thought. And how many of all the Odes called his, more and fewer in various Copies, do you yourself care to deal with?—And in the better ones how often some lines, as I think for this reason, unworthy of the Rest—interpolated perhaps from the Mouths of his many Devotees, Mystical and Sensual—or crept into Manuscripts of which he never arranged or corrected one from the First?

This, together with the confined Action of Persian Grammar, whose organic simplicity seems to me its difficulty when applied, makes the Line by Line Translation of a Poem not line by line precious tedious in proportion to its length. Especially— (what the Sonnet does not feel)—in the Narrative; which I found when once eased in its Collar, and yet missing somewhat of rhythmical Amble, somehow, and not without resistance on my part, swerved into that "easy road" of Verse—easiest as unbeset with any exigencies of Rhyme. Those little Stories, too, which you thought untractable, but which have their Use as well as Humour by way of quaint Interlude Music between the little Acts, felt ill at ease in solemn Lowth-Isaiah Prose, and had learn'd their tune, you know, before even Hiawatha came to teach people to quarrel about it. Till, one part drawing on another, the Whole grew to the present form.

As for the much bodily omitted—it may be readily guessed that an Asiatic of the 15th Century might say much on such a subject that an Englishman of the 19th would not care to read. Not that our Jámi is ever *licentious* like his Contemporary Chaucer, nor like Chaucer's Posterity in Times that called themselves more Civil. But better Men will not now endure a simplicity of Speech that Worse men abuse. Then the many more, and foolisher, Stories— preliminary Te Deums to Allah and Allah's-shadow Sháh—very much about Alef Noses, Eyebrows like inverted Núns, drunken Narcissus Eyes—and that eternal Moon Face which never wanes from Persia—of all which there is surely enough in this Glimpse of the Original. No doubt some Oriental character escapes—the Story sometimes becomes too Skin and Bone without due interval of even Stupid and Bad. Of the two Evils?—At least what I have chosen is least in point of bulk; scarcely in proportion with the length of its Apology which, as usual, probably discharges one's own Conscience at too great a Price; people at once turning against you the Arms they might have wanted had you not laid them down. However it may be with this, I am sure a complete Translation—even in Prose—would not have been a readable one—which, after all, is a useful property of most Books, even of Poetry.

In studying the Original, you know, one gets contentedly carried over barren Ground in a new Land of Language—excited by chasing any new Game that will but show Sport; the most worthless to win asking perhaps all the sharper Energy to pursue, and so far yielding all the more Satisfaction when run down. Especially, cheer'd on as I was by such a Huntsman as poor Dog of a Persian Scholar never hunted with before; and moreover—but that

was rather in the Spanish Sierras—by the Presence
of a Lady in the Field, silently brightening about
us like Aurora's Self, or chiming in with musical
Encouragement that all we started and ran down
must be Royal Game!

Ah, happy Days! When shall we Three meet
again—when dip in that unreturning Tide of Time
and Circumstance!—In those Meadows far from the
World, it seemed, as Salámán's Island—before an
Iron Railway broke the Heart of that Happy Valley
whose Gossip was the Millwheel, and Visitors the
Summer Airs that momentarily ruffled the sleepy
Stream that turned it as they chased one another
over to lose themselves in Whispers in the Copse
beyond. Or returning—I suppose you remember
whose Lines they are

> When Winter Skies were ting'd with Crimson still
> Where Thornbush nestles on the quiet hill,
> And the live Amber round the setting Sun,
> Lighting the Labourer home whose Work is done,
> Burn'd like a Golden Angel-ground above
> The solitary Home of Peace and Love—

at such an hour drawing home together for a
fireside Night of it with Aeschylus or Calderon in
the Cottage, whose walls, modest almost as those
of the Poor who cluster'd—and with good reason—
round, make to my Eyes the Tower'd Crown of

Oxford hanging in the Horizon, and with all Honour won, but a dingy Vapour in Comparison. And now, should they beckon from the terrible Ganges, and this little Book begun as a happy Record of past, and pledge perhaps of Future, Fellowship in Study, darken already with the shadow of everlasting Farewell!

But to turn from you Two to a Public—nearly as numerous—(with whom, by the way, this Letter may die without a name that *you* know very well how to supply),—here is the best I could make of Jámi's Poem—"Ouvrage de peu d'étendue," says the Biographie Universelle, and, whatever that means, here collaps'd into a nutshell Epic indeed; whose Story however, if nothing else, may interest some Scholars as one of Persian Mysticism—perhaps the grand Mystery of all Religions—an Allegory fairly devised and carried out—dramatically culminating as it goes on; and told as to this day the East loves to tell her Story, illustrated by Fables and Tales, so often (as we read in the latest Travels) at the expense of the poor Arab of the Desert.

The Proper Names—and some other Words peculiar to the East—are printed as near as may be to their native shape and sound—"Sulayman" for Solomon "Yúsuf" for Joseph, etc., as being not only more musical, but retaining their Oriental flavour unalloyed with European Association. The *accented* Vowels are to be pronounced long, as in Italian—Salámán—Absál—Shírín, etc.

The Original is in rhymed Couplets of this measure:—

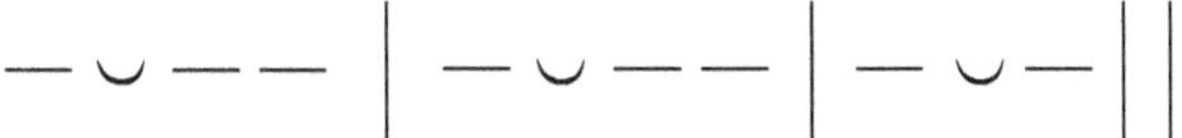

which those who like Monkish Latin may remember in:—

> Duc Salámán verba Regis cogitat,
> Pectus intrá de profundis aestuat.

or in English—by way of asking, "your Clemency for us and for our Tragedy"—

> "Of Salámán and of Absál hear the Song;
> Little wants Man here below, nor little long."

Prologue

Translated from the Persian of JÁMÍ

I

Oh Thou whose Memory quickens Lovers'
    Souls,
Whose Fount of Joy renews the Lover's
    Tongue,
Thy Shadow falls across the World, and They
Bow down to it; and of the Rich in Beauty
Thou art the Riches that make Lovers mad.
Not till thy Secret Beauty through the Cheek
Of Laila smite does she inflame Majnún,[1]
And not till Thou have sugar'd Shírín's Lip
The Hearts of those Two Lovers fill with
    Blood.[2]
For Lov'd and Lover are not but by Thee,
Nor Beauty;—Mortal Beauty but the Veil

---

1 All well-known Types of Eastern Lovers. Shírín and her Suitors
   figure in Section XX.
2 The Persian Mystics also represent the Deity Diceing with Human
   Destiny behind the Curtain.

Thy Heavenly hides behind, and from itself
Feeds, and our Hearts yearn after as a Bride
That glances past us Veil'd—but ever so
As none the Beauty from the Veil may know.
How long wilt thou continue thus the World
To cozen with the Fantom of a Veil
From which Thou only peepest?—Time it is
To unfold thy perfect Beauty. I would be
Thy Lover, and Thine only—I, mine Eyes
Seal'd in the Light of Thee to all but Thee,
Yea, in the Revelation of Thyself
Self-Lost, and Conscience-quit of Good and
     Evil.
Thou movest under all the Forms of Truth,
Under the Forms of all Created Things;
Look whence I will, still nothing I discern
But Thee in all the Universe, in which
Thyself Thou dost invest, and through the
     Eyes
Of Man, the subtle Censor[3] scrutinize.
To thy Harím Dividuality
No Entrance finds—no Word of THIS and
     THAT;
Do Thou my separate and Derivéd Self
Make one with thy Essential! Leave me room

------

3 The Appolonius of Keat's *Lamnia*.

On that Diván which leaves no Room for
    Two;[4]
Lest, like the Simple Kurd of whom they tell,
I grow perplext, Oh God! 'twixt "I" and
    "Thou;"
If *I*—this Dignity and Wisdom whence?
If *Thou*—then what this abject Impotence?

A Kurd perplext by Fortune's Frolics
Left his Desert for the City.
Sees a City full of Noise and
Clamour, agitated People,
Hither, Thither, Back and Forward
Running, some intent on Travel,
Others home again returning,
Right to Left, and Left to Right,
Life-disquiet everywhere!
Kurd, when he beholds the Turmoil,
Creeps aside, and, Travel-weary,
Fain would go to Sleep; "But," saith he,

---

4 This Súfi Identification with Deity (further illustrated in the Story
of Section XIX) is shadowed in a Parable of Jeláddín, of which
here is an outline. "One knocked at the Belov'd's Door; and a
Voice asked from within, 'Who is there?' and he answered, 'It is I'.
Then the Voice said, 'This house will not hold ME and THEE'. And
the Door was not opened. Then went the Lover into the Desert,
and fasted and prayed in Solitude. And after a Year he returned
and knocked again at the Door. And again the Voice said, 'Who is
there?' and he said, 'It is Thyself!'—and the Door was opened to
him."

"How shall I in all this Hubbub
"Know myself again on waking?"
So by way of Recognition
Ties a Pumpkin round his Foot,
And turns to Sleep. A Knave that heard him
Crept behind, and slily watching
Slips the Pumpkin off the Sleeper's
Ancle, ties it round his own,
And so down to sleep beside him.
By and by the Kurd awaking
Looks directly for his Signal—
Sees it on another's Ancle—
Cries aloud, "Oh Good-for-Nothing
Rascal to perplex me so!
That by you I am bewilder'd,
Whether I be I or no!
If I—the Pumpkin why on You?
If You—then Where am I, and Who?"

Oh God! this poor bewilder'd Kurd am I,
Than any Kurd more helpless!—Oh, do thou
Strike down a Ray of Light into my
    Darkness!
Turn by thy Grace these Dregs into pure
    Wine,
To recreate the Spirits of the Good!
Or if not that, yet, as the little Cup

Whose Name I go by,[5] not unworthy found
I listen in the Tavern of Sweet Songs,
And catch no Echo of their Harmony:
The Guests have drunk the Wine and are
    departed,
Leaving their empty Bowls behind—not one
To carry on the Revel Cup in hand!
Up Jámí then! and whether Lees or Wine
To offer—boldly offer it in Thine!

II

And yet how long, Jámí, in this Old House
Stringing thy Pearls upon a Harp of Song?
Year after Year striking up some new Song,
The Breath of some Old Story?[6] Life is gone,
And yet the Song is not the Last; my Soul
Is spent—and still a Story to be told!
And I, whose Back is crookéd as the Harp
I still keep tuning through the Night till
    Day!
That Harp untun'd by Time—the Harper's
    hand

---

5   The Poet's name "Jámí", also signifying "A Cup". The Poet's
    "Yúsuf and Zulaikha" opens also with this Divine Wine, the
    favourite symbol of Háfiz and other Persian Mystics. The Tavern
    spoken of is The World.
6   "Yúsuf and Zulaikha", and "Laila and Majnún", etc.

Shaking with Age—how shall the Harper's hand
Repair its cunning, and the sweet old Harp
Be modulated as of old? Methinks
'Tis time to break and cast it in the Fire;
Yea, sweet the Harp that can be sweet no more,
To cast it in the Fire—the vain old Harp
That can no more sound Sweetness to the Ear,
But burn'd may breathe sweet Attar to the
  Soul,
And comfort so the Faith and Intellect,
Now that the Body looks to Dissolution.
My Teeth fall out—my two Eyes see no more
Till by Feringhi Glasses turn'd to Four;[7]
Pain sits with me sitting behind my knees,
From which I hardly rise unhelpt of hand;
I bow down to my Root, and like a Child
Yearn, as is likely, to my Mother Earth,
With whom I soon shall cease to moan and
  weep,
And on my Mother's Bosom fall asleep.
The House in Ruin, and its Music heard
No more within, nor at the Door of Speech,
Better in Silence and Oblivion
To fold me Head and Foot, remembering
What that BELOVED to the Master
  whisper'd:—

---

7 First notice of Spectacles in Oriental Poetry, perhaps.

"No longer think of Rhyme, but think of
    Me!"—
Of Whom?—of Him whose Palace The Soul
    is,
And Treasure-House—who notices and knows
Its Income and Out-going, and *then* comes
To fill it when the Stranger is departed.
Whose Shadow being Kings—whose Attributes
The Type of Theirs—their Wrath and Favour
    His
Lo! in the Celebration of His Glory.
The King Himself[8] come on me unaware,
And suddenly arrests me for his own.
Wherefore once more I take—best quitted else
The Field of Verse, to chaunt that double
    Praise,
And in that Memory refresh my Soul
Until I grasp the Skirt of Living Presence.

One who travel'd in the Desert
Saw Majnún where he was sitting
All alone like a Magician
Tracing Letters in the Sand.
"Oh distracted Lover! writing
What the Sword-wind of the Desert

---

8 "The Master," whose Verse is quoted, is Jellalladdín, the Great
  Súfí Teacher. The "King Himself" is Yacúb Beg, whose Father's
  Vision appears in the next Section.

Undecyphers soon as written,
So that none who travels after
Shall be able to interpret!"—
Majnún answer'd, "I am writing
'LAILI'—were it only 'LAILI,'
Yet a Book of Love and Passion;
And, with but her Name to dote on,
Amorously I caress it
As it were Herself, and sip
Her Presence till I drink her Lip."

III

When Night had thus far brought me with my
   Book,
In middle Thought Sleep robb'd me of myself;
And in a Dream Myself I seem'd to see,
Walking along a straight and even Road,
And clean as is the Soul of the Súfí;
A Road whose spotless Surface neither Breeze
Lifted in Dust, nor mix'd the Rain to Mire.
There I, methought, was pacing tranquilly,
When, on a sudden, the tumultuous Shout
Of Soldiery behind broke on mine Ear,
And took away my Wit and Strength for Fear.
I look'd about for Refuge, and Behold!
A Palace was before me; whither running

For Refuge from the coming Soldiery,
Suddenly from the Troop a Sháhzemán,[9]
By Name and Nature HASAN—on the Horse
Of Honour mounted—robed in Royal Robes,
And wearing a White Turban on his Head,
Turn'd his Rein tow'rd me, and with smiling
   Lips
Open'd before my Eyes the Door of Peace.
Then, riding up to me, dismounted; kiss'd
My Hand, and did me Courtesy; and I,
How glad of his Protection, and the Grace
He gave it with!—Who then of gracious Speech
Many a Jewel utter'd; but of these
Not one that in my Ear till Morning hung.
When, waking on my Bed, my waking Wit
I question'd what the Vision meant, it
   answered;
"This Courtesy and Favour of the Shah
Foreshadows the fair Acceptance of thy Verse,
Which lose no moment pushing to
   Conclusion."
This hearing, I address'd me like a Pen
To steady Writing; for perchance, I thought,

---

9 "Lord of the World, SOVEREIGN; HASAN, BEAUTIFUL, GOOD."
HASSAN BEG of Western Persia, famous for his Beauty, had helped
Jámí with Escort in a dangerous Pilgrimage. He died (as History
and a previous line in the Oriental tell) before *Salámán* was
written, and was succeeded by his son Yácúb.

From the same Fountain whence the Vision
  grew
The Interpretation also may come True.

    Breathless ran a simple Rustic
    To a Cunning Man of Dreams;
    "Lo, this Morning I was dreaming—
    And methought, in yon deserted
    Village wander'd—all about me
    Shatter'd Houses—and, Behold!
    Into one, methought, I went—and
    Search'd—and found a Hoard of Gold!"
    Quoth the Prophet in Derision,
    "Oh Thou Jewel of Creation,
    Go and sole your Feet like Horse's,
    And returning to your Village
    Stamp and scratch with Hoof and Nail,
    And give Earth so sound a Shaking,
    She must hand you something up."
    Went at once the unsuspecting
    Countryman; with hearty Purpose
    Set to work as he was told;
    And, the very first Encounter,
    Struck upon his Hoard of Gold!

Until Thou hast thy Purpose by the Hilt,
Catch at it boldly—or Thou never wilt.

The Story

IV

A SHAH there was who ruled the Realm of
　Yún,[1]
And wore the Ring of Empire of Sikander;
And in his Reign A SAGE, who had the Tower
Of Wisdom of so strong Foundation built
That Wise Men from all Quarters of the World
To catch the Word of Wisdom from his Lip
Went in a Girdle round him.—Which THE
　SHAH
Observing, took him to his Secresy;
Stirr'd not a Step nor set Design afoot
Without that Sage's sanction; till, so counsel'd,
From Káf to Káf[2] reach'd his Dominion:
No Nation of the World or Nation's Chief
Who wore the Ring but under span of his

1　Yún—or "YAVAN," Son of Japhet, from whom the Country was
　called "YÚNAN,"—IONIA, meant by the Persians to express Greece
　generally. Sikander is, of course, Alexander the Great, of whose
　Ethics Jámí wrote, as Nizami of his Deeds.
2　Káf.—the Fabulous Mountain supposed by Asiatics to surround
　the World, binding the Horizon on all sides.

Bow'd down the Neck; then rising up in Peace
Under his Justice grew, and knew no Wrong,
And in their Strength was his Dominion
    Strong.
The SHAH that has not Wisdom in Himself,
Nor has a Wise Man for his Counsellor,
The Wand of his Authority falls short,
And his Dominion crumbles at the Base.
For he, discerning not the Characters
Of Tyranny and Justice, confounds both,
Making the World a Desert, and the Fount
Of Justice a Seráb.[3] Well was it said,
"Better just Káfir than Believing Tyrant."

> *"God said to the Prophet David,—*
> *David, speak, and to the Challenge*
> *Answer of the Faith within Thee.*
> *Even Unbelieving Princes,*
> *Ill-reported if Unworthy,*
> *Yet, if They be Just and Righteous,*
> *Were their Worship of* THE FIRE—
> *Even These unto Themselves*
> *Reap glory and redress the World."*

---

3 Miráge; but, of two Foreign Words, why not the more original
   Persian?—identical with the Hebrew Sháráb; as in Isaiah xv. 7;
   "The *Sháráb* (or *Miráge*) shall become a Lake;"—rather, and
   better, than our Version, "The parched Ground shall become a
   Pool."—*See* Gesenius.

V

One Night THE SHAH of Yúnan, as his wont,
Consider'd of his Power, and told his State,
How great it was, and how about him sat
The Robe of Honour of Prosperity;
Then found he nothing wanted to his Heart,
Unless a Son, who his Dominion
And Glory might inherit after him.
And then he turn'd him to THE SHAH, and
    said;
"Oh Thou, whose Wisdom is the Rule of
    Kings—
(Glory to God who gave it!)—answer me;
Is any Blessing better than a Son?
Man's prime Desire; by which his Name and
    He
Shall live beyond Himself; by whom his Eyes
Shine living, and his Dust with Roses blows;
A Foot for Thee to stand on, he shall be
A Hand to stop thy Falling; in his Youth
Thou shalt be Young, and in his Strength be
    Strong;
Sharp shall he be in Battle as a Sword,
A Cloud of Arrows on the Enemy's Head;
His Voice shall cheer his Friends to Plight,
And turn the Foeman's Glory into Flight."

Thus much of a Good Son, whose wholesome
    Growth
Approves the Root he grew from; but for one
Kneaded of Evil—Well, could one undo
His Generation, and as early pull
Him and his Vices from the String of Time.
Like Noah's, puff'd with Ignorance and Pride,
Who felt the Stab of "HE IS NONE OF
    THINE!"
And perish'd in the Deluge.[4] And because
All are not Good, be slow to pray for One,
Whom having you may have to pray to lose.

---

4 In the Kurán God engaged to save Noah and his Family—meaning
all who believed in the Warning. One of Noah's Sons (Canaan or
Yam, some think) would not believe. "And the Ark swam with
them between waves like Mountains, and Noah called up to
his Son, who was separated from him, saying, 'Embark with us,
my Son, and stay not with the Unbelievers.' He answered, 'I will
get on a Mountain which will secure me from the Water.' Noah
replied, 'There is no security this Day from the Decree of God,
except for him on whom he shall have Mercy.' And a Wave passed
between them, and he became one of those who were drowned.
And it was said, 'Oh Earth, swallow up thy waters, and Thou, oh
Heaven, withhold thy Rain!' And immediately the Water abated
and the Decree was fulfilled, and the Ark rested on the Mountain
Al Judi, and it was said, 'Away with the ungodly People!'—Noah
called upon his Lord and said, 'Oh Lord, verily my Son is of
my Family, and thy Promise is True; for Thou art of those who
exercise Judgment.' God answered, 'Oh Noah, verily he is not of
thy Family; this intercession of thine for him is not a righteous
work.'"—*Sale's Kurán*, Vol. II. p. 21.

Crazy for the Curse of Children,
Ran before the Sheikh a Fellow,
Crying out, "Oh hear and help me!
Pray to Allah from my Clay
To raise me up a fresh young Cypress,
Who my Childless Eyes may lighten
With the Beauty of his Presence."
Said the Sheikh, "Be wise, and leave it
Wholly in the Hand of Allah,
Who, whatever we are after,
Understands our Business best."
But the Man persisted, saying,
"Sheikh, I languish in my Longing;
Help, and set my Prayer a-going!"
Then the Sheikh held up his Hand—
Pray'd—his Arrow flew to Heaven—
From the Hunting-ground of Darkness
Down a musky Fawn of China
Brought—a Boy—who, when the Tender
Shoot of Passion in him planted
Found sufficient Soil and Sap,
Took to Drinking with his Fellows;
From a Corner of the House-top
Ill affronts a Neighbour's Wife,
Draws his Dagger on the Husband,
Who complains before the Justice,
And the Father has to pay.

Day and Night the Youngster's Doings
Such—the Talk of all the City;
Nor Entreaty, Threat, or Counsel
Held him; till the Desperate Father
Once more to the Sheikh a-running,
Catches at his Garment, crying—
"Sheikh, my only Hope and Helper!
One more Prayer! that God who laid
Will take that Trouble from my Head!"
But the Sheikh replied: "Remember
How that very Day I warn'd you
Better not importune Allah;
Unto whom remains no other
Prayer, unless to pray for Pardon.
When from this World we are summon'd
On to bind the pack of Travel
Son or Daughter ill shall help us;
Slaves we are, and unencumber'd
Best may do the Master's mind;
And, whatever he may order,
Do it with a Will Resign'd."

VI

When the Sharp-witted SAGE
Had heard these Sayings of THE SHAH, he
  said,

"Oh SHAH, who would not be the Slave of
    Lust
Must still endure the Sorrow of no Son.
—Lust that makes blind the Reason; Lust that
    makes
A Devil's self seem Angel to our Eyes;
A Cataract that, carrying havoc with it,
Confounds the prosperous House; a Road of
    Mire
Where whoso falls he rises not again;
A Wine of which whoever tastes shall see
Redemption's face no more—one little Sip
Of that delicious and unlawful Drink
Making crave much, and hanging round the
    Palate
Till it become a Ring to lead thee by[5]
(Putting the rope in a Vain Woman's hand),
Till thou thyself go down the Way of Nothing.
"For what is Woman? A Foolish, Faithless
    Thing
To whom The Wise Self-subjected, himself
Deep sinks beneath the Folly he sets up.
A very Káfir in Rapacity;
Clothe her a hundred Years in Gold and Jewel,
Her Garment with Brocade of Susa braided,

---

5 "*Mihar*," a Piece of Wood put through a Camel's Nose to guide
   him by.

Her very Night-gear wrought in Cloth of
    Gold,
Dangle her Ears with Ruby and with Pearl,
Her House with Golden Vessels all a-blaze,
Her Tables loaded with the Fruit of Kings,
Ispahan Apples, Pomegranates of Yazd;
And, be she thirsty, from a Jewell'd Cup
Drinking the Water of the Well of Life
One little twist of Temper,—all you've done
Goes all for Nothing. 'Torment of my Life!'
She cries, 'What have you ever done for me!'—
Her Brow's white Tablet—Yes—'tis uninscrib'd
With any Letter of Fidelity;
Who ever read it there? Lo, in your Bosom
She lies for Years—you turn away a moment,
And she forgets you—worse, if as you turn
Her Eye should light on any Younger Lover."

Once upon the Throne of Judgment,
Telling one another Secrets,
Sat SULAYMAN and BALKÍS;[6]
The Hearts of Both were turn'd to Truth,
Unsullied by Deception.
First the King of Faith SULAYMAN
Spoke—"Though mine the Ring of Empire,
Never any Day that passes

---

6 Solomon and the Queen of Sheba.

Darkens any one my Door-way
But into his Hand I look
And He who comes not empty-handed
Grows to Honour in mine Eyes."
After this BALKÍS *a Secret*
From her hidden Bosom utter'd,
Saying—"Never Night or Morning
Comely Youth before me passes
Whom I look not longing after;
Saying to myself, 'Oh were he
Comforting of my Sick Soul!—'"

"If this, as wise Ferdúsi says, the Curse
Of Better Women, what should be the Worse?"

VII

THE SAGE his Satire ended; and THE SHAH
With Magic-mighty WISDOM his pure WILL
Leaguing, its Self-fulfilment wrought from
    Heaven.
And Lo! from Darkness came to Light A
    CHILD,
Of Carnal Composition Unattaint,—
A Rosebud blowing on the Royal Stem,—
A Perfume from the Realm of Wisdom wafted;
The Crowning Jewel of the Crown; a Star

Under whose Augury triumph'd the Throne.
For whose Auspicious Name they clove the
      Words
"SALÁMAT"—Incolumity from Evil—
And "AUSEMÁN"—the Heav'n from which he
      came
And hail'd him by the title of SALÁMÁN.
And whereas from no Mother Milk he drew,
They chose for him a Nurse—her name
      ABSÁL—
Her Years not Twenty—from the Silver Line
Dividing the Musk-Harvest of her Hair
Down to her Foot that trampled Crowns of
      Kings,
A Moon of Beauty Full; who thus elect
SALÁMÁN of Auspicious Augury
Should carry in the Garment of her Bounty,
Should feed Him with the Flowing of her
      Breast.
As soon as she had opened Eyes on him
She closed those Eyes to all the World beside,
And her Soul crazed, a-doting on her Jewel,
Her Jewel in a Golden Cradle set;
Opening and shutting which her Day's Delight,
To gaze upon his Heart-inflaming Cheek,
Upon the Darling whom, could she, she would

Have cradled as the Baby of her Eye.[7]
In Rose and Musk she wash'd him—to his Lips
Press'd the pure Sugar from the Honeycomb;
And when, Day over, she withdrew her Milk,
She made, and having laid him in, his Bed,
Burn'd all Night like a Taper o'er his Head.
Then still as Morning came, and as he grew,
She dress'd him like a Little Idol up;
On with his Robe—with fresh Collyrium Dew
Touch'd his Narcissus Eyes—the Musky Locks
Divided from his Forehead—and embraced
With Gold and Ruby Girdle his fine Waist.—
So rear'd she him till full Fourteen his Years,
Fourteen-day full the Beauty of his Face,
That rode high in a Hundred Thousand Hearts;
Yea, when SALÁMÁN was but Half-lance high,
Lance-like he struck a wound in every One,
And burn'd and shook down Splendour like a
    Sun.

VIII

Soon as the Lord of Heav'n had sprung his
    Horse
Over the Horizon into the Blue Field,

---

7 Literally, *Mardumak*—the *Mannikin*, Or *Pupil*, of the Eye, corre-
  sponding to the Image so frequently used by our old Poets.

Salámán rose drunk with the Wine of Sleep,
And set himself a-stirrup for the Field;
He and a Troop of Princes—Kings in Blood,
Kings too in the Kingdom-troubling Tribe of
    Beauty,
All Young in Years and Courage,[8] Bat in hand
Gallop'd a-field, toss'd down the Golden Ball
And chased, so many Crescent Moons a Full;
And, all alike Intent upon the Game,
SALÁMÁN still would carry from them all
The Prize, and shouting "Hál!" drive Home
    the Ball.[9]
This done, Salámán bent him as a Bow
To Shooting—from the Marksmen of the World
Call'd for an unstrung Bow—himself the Cord
Fitted unhelpt,[10] and nimbly with his hand
Twanging made cry, and drew it to his Ear:

8 The same Persian Word serving for Both.

9 The Game of Chúgán, for Centuries the Royal Game of Persia,
   and adopted (Ouseley thinks) under varying modifications of
   Name and Practice by other Nations, was played by Horsemen,
   who, suitably habited, and armed with semicircular-headed Bats
   or Sticks so short the Player must stoop below the Saddle-bow to
   strike, strove to drive a Ball through a Goal of upright Pillars. *See*
   Appendix.

10 Bows being so gradually stiffened, to the Age and Strength of
   the Archer, as at last to need five Hundredweight of Pressure to
   bend, says an old Translation of Chardin, who describes all the
   Process up to bringing up the String to the Ear, "*as if to hang it
   there*" before Shooting. Then the First Trial was, who could shoot
   highest; then, the Mark, etc.

Then, fixing the Three-feather'd Fowl,
    discharged.
No point in Heaven's Azure but his Arrow
Hit; nay, but Heaven were made of Adamant,
Would overtake the Horizon as it roll'd;
And, whether aiming at the Fawn a-foot,
Or Bird on wing, his Arrow went away
Straight—like the Soul that cannot go astray.
When Night came, that releases Man from
    Toil,
He play'd the Chess of Social Intercourse;
Prepared his Banquet Hall like Paradise,
Summon'd his Houri-faced Musicians,
And, when his Brain grew warm with Wine,
    the Veil
Flung off him of Reserve. Now Lip to Lip
Concerting with the Singer he would breathe
Like a Messias Life into the Dead;
Now made of the Melodious-moving Pipe
A Sugar-cane between his Lips that ran
Men's Ears with Sweetness: Taking up a Harp,
Between its dry String and his Finger fresh
As if a little Child for Chastisement,
Pinching its Ear such Cries of Sorrow wrung
As drew Blood to the Eyes of Older Men.
Now sang He like the Nightingale alone,
Now set together Voice and Instrument;

And thus with his Associates Night he spent.
His Soul rejoiced in Knowledge of all kinds;
The fine Edge of his Wit would split a Hair,
And in the Noose of Apprehension catch
A Meaning ere articulate in Word;
His Verse was like the PLEIADS;[11] his Discourse
The MOURNERS OF THE BIER; his Penmanship,
(Tablet and running Reed his Worshippers,)
Fine on the Lip of Youth as the First Hair,
Drove PENMEN, as with LOVERS, to Despair.
His Bounty was as Ocean's—nay, the Sea's
Self but the Foam of his Munificence,
For it threw up the Shell, but he the Pearl;
He was a Cloud that rain'd upon the World
Dirhems for Drops; the Banquet of whose
    Bounty
Left Hátim's[12] Churlish in Comparison—

IX

Suddenly that Sweet Minister of mine
Rebuked me angrily; "What Folly, Jámí,

---

11 i.e. compactly strung, as opposed to Discursive Rhetoric, which is
   compared to the scattered Stars of THE BIER and its MOURNERS,
   or what we call THE GREAT BEAR. This contrast is otherwise
   prettily applied in the Anvari Soheili—"When one grows poor,
   his Friends, heretofore compact as THE PLEIADS, disperse wide
   asunder as THE MOURNERS."
12 The Persian Type of Liberality, infinitely celebrated.

Wearing that indefatigable Pen
In celebration of an Alien SHAH
Whose Throne, not grounded in the Eternal
     World,
YESTERDAY was, TO-DAY is not!"[13] I answer'd;
"Oh Fount of Light!—under an Alien Name
I shadow One upon whose Head the Crown
Both WAS and IS TO-DAY; to whose Firmán
The Seven Kingdoms of the World are subject,
And the Seas Seven but droppings of his
     Largess.
Good luck to him who under other Name
Taught us to veil the Praises of a Power
To which the Initiate scarce find open Door."

Sat a Lover solitary
Self-discoursing in a Corner,
Passionate and ever-changing
Invocation pouring out;
Sometimes Sun and Moon; and sometimes
Under Hyacinth half-hidden
Roses; or the lofty Cypress,
And the little Weed below.
Nightingaling thus a Noodle
Heard him, and, completely puzzled,—

---

13 The Hero of the Story being of YÚNAN—IONIA, or GREECE
   generally, (the Persian Geography not being very precise,)—and
   so not of THE FAITH.

"What!" quoth he, "And you, a Lover,
Raving not about your Mistress,
But about the Moon and Roses!"
Answer'd he; "Oh thou that aimest
Wide of Love, and Lover's Language
Wholly misinterpreting;
Sun and Moon are but my Lady's
Self, as any Lover knows;
Hyacinth I said, and meant her
Hair—her Cheek was in the Rose—
And I myself the wretched Weed
That in her Cypress Shadow grows."

X

Now was SALÁMÁN in his Prime of Growth,
His Cypress Stature risen to high Top,
And the new-blooming Garden of his Beauty
Began to bear; and ABSÁL long'd to gather;
But the Fruit grew upon too high a Bough,
To which the Noose of her Desire was short.
She too rejoiced in Beauty of her own
No whit behind SALÁMÁN, whom she now
Began enticing with her Sorcery.
Now from her Hair would twine a musky
  Chain,
To bind his Heart—now twist it into Curls

Nestling innumerable Temptations;
Doubled the Darkness of her Eyes with Surma
To make him lose his way, and over them
Adorn'd the Bows[14] that were to shoot him
    then;
Now to the Rose-leaf of her Cheek would add
Fresh Rose, and then a Grain of Musk[15] lay
    there,
The Bird of the Belovéd Heart to snare.
Now with a Laugh would break the Ruby
    Seal
That lockt up Pearl; or busied in the Room
Would smite her Hand perhaps—on that
    pretence
To lift and show the Silver in her Sleeve;
Or hastily rising clash her Golden Anclets
To draw the Crownéd Head under her Feet.
Thus by innumerable Bridal wiles
She went about soliciting his Eyes,
Which she would scarce let lose her for a
    Moment;
For well she knew that mainly by THE EYE
Love makes his Sign, and by no other Road
Enters and takes possession of the Heart.

---

14 With dark Indigo Paint, as the Archery Bow with a thin Papyrus-
    like Bark.
15 A Patch,' sc.—"*Noir comme le Musc.*"—De Sacy.

Burning with Desire ZULAIKHA
Built a Chamber, Wall and Ceiling
Blank as an untarnisht Mirror,
Spotless as the Heart of YÚSUF.
Then she made a cunning Painter
Multiply her Image round it;
Not an Inch of Wall but echoed
With the Reflex of her Beauty.
Then amid them all in all her
Glory sat she down, and sent for
YÚSUF—she began a Tale
Of Love—and Lifted up her Veil.
From her Look he turn'd, but turning
Wheresoever, ever saw her
Looking, looking at him still.
Then Desire arose within him—
He was almost yielding—almost
Laying Honey on her Lip—
When a Signal out of Darkness
Spoke to him—and he withdrew
His Hand, and dropt the Skirt of Fortune.

XI

Thus day by day did ABSÁL tempt
    SALÁMÁN,
And by and bye her Wiles began to work.

Her Eyes Narcissus stole his Sleep—their
   Lashes
Pierc'd to his Heart—out from her Locks a
   Snake
Bit him—and bitter, bitter on his Tongue
Became the Memory of her honey Lip.
He saw the Ringlet restless on her Cheek,
And he too quiver'd with Desire; his Tears
Turn'd Crimson from her Cheek, whose
   musky spot
Infected all his soul with Melancholy.
Love drew him from behind the Veil, where yet
Withheld him better Resolution-
"Oh, should the Food I long for, tasted, turn
Unwholesome, and if all my Life to come
Should sicken from one momentary Sweet!"

On the Sea-shore sat a Raven,
Blind, and from the bitter Cistern
Forc'd his only Drink to draw.
Suddenly the Pelican
Flying over Fortune's Shadow
Cast upon his Head,[16] and calling—
"Come, poor Son of Salt, and taste of
Sweet, sweet Water from my Maw."
Said the Raven, "If I taste it

---

16 Alluding to the Phœnix, the Shadow of whose wings foretold a
   Crown upon the Head it passed over.

Once, the Salt I have to live on
May for ever turn to Loathing;
And I sit a Bird accurst
Upon the Shore to die of Thirst."

XII

Now when SALÁMÁN's Heart turn'd to ABSÁL,
Her Star was happy in the Heavens—Old Love
Put forth afresh—Desire doubled his Bond:
And of the running Time she watch'd an Hour
To creep into the Mansion of her Moon
And satiate her soul upon his Lips.
And the Hour came; she stole into his
    Chamber
Ran up to him, Life's offer in her Hand—
And, falling like a Shadow at his Feet,
She laid her Face beneath. SALÁMÁN then
With all the Courtesies of Princely Grace
Put forth his Hand—he rais'd her in his Arms
He held her trembling there—and from that
    Fount
Drew first Desire; then Deeper from her Lips,
That, yielding, mutually drew from his
A Wine that ever drawn from never fail'd—
So through the Day—so through another
    still—

The Day became a Seventh—the Seventh a
   Moon—
The Moon a Year—while they rejoiced
   together,
Thinking their Pleasure never was to end.
But rolling Heaven whisper'd from his
   Ambush,
"So in my License is it not set down.
Ah for the sweet Societies I make
At Morning and before the Nightfall break;
Ah for the Bliss that with the Setting Sun
I mix, and, with his Rising, all is done!"

Into Baghdad came a hungry
Arab—after many days of waiting
In to the Khalífah's Supper
Push'd, and got before a Pasty
Luscious as the Lip of Beauty,
Or the Tongue of Eloquence.
Soon as seen, Indecent Hunger
Seizes up and swallows down;
Then his mouth undaunted wiping—
"Oh Khalífah, hear me Swear,
Not of any other Pasty
Than of Thine to sup or dine."
The Khalífah laugh'd and answer'd;
"Fool! who thinkest to determine

What is in the Hands of Fate—
Take and thrust him from the Gate!"

XIII

While a Full Year was counted by the Moon,
SALÁMÁN and ABSÁL rejoiced together,
And for so long he stood not in the face
Of SAGE or SHAH, and their bereavéd Hearts
Were torn in twain with the Desire of Him.
They question'd those about him, and from
    them
Heard something; then Himself in Presence
    summon'd,
And, subtly sifting on all sides, so plied
Interrogation till it hit the Mark,
And all the Truth was told. Then SAGE and
    SHAH
Struck out with Hand and Foot in his Redress.
And First with REASON, which is also Best;
REASON that rights the Retrograde—completes
The Imperfect—REASON that unties the Knot:
For REASON is the Fountain from of old
From which the Prophets drew, and none
    beside.
Who boasts of other Inspiration lies—
There are no other Prophets than The Wise.

XIV

First spoke THE SHAH;—"SALÁMÁN, Oh my
    Soul,
Oh Taper of the Banquet of my House,
Light of the Eyes of my Prosperity,
And making bloom the Court of Hope with
    Rose;
Years Rose-bud-like my own Blood devour'd
Till in my hand I carried thee, my Rose;
Oh do not tear my Garment from my Hand,
Nor wound thy Father with a Dagger Thorn.
Years for thy sake the Crown has worn my
    Brow,
And Years my Foot been growing to the
    Throne
Only for Thee—Oh spurn them not with
    Thine;
Oh turn thy Face from Dalliance unwise,
Lay not thy Heart's hand on a Minion!
For what thy Proper Pastime? Is it not
To mount and manage RAKHSH[17] along the
    Field;
Not, with no stouter weapon than a Love-
    lock,
Idly reclining on a Silver Breast.

---

17 "LIGHTNING." The name of RUSTAM's famous Horse in the SHAH-
NAMEH.

Go, fly thine Arrow at the Antelope
And Lion—let not me my Lion see
Slain by the Arrow eyes of a Ghazal.
Go, flash thy Steel among the Ranks of Men,
And smite the Warriors' Necks; not, flying
    them,
Lay down thine own beneath a Woman's Foot.
Leave off such doing in the Name of God,
Nor bring thy Father weeping to the Ground;
Years have I held myself aloft, and all
For Thee—Oh Shame if thou prepare my Fall!"

When before Shirúeh's Feet
Drencht in Blood fell KAI KHUSRAU,[18]
He declared this Parable—
"Wretch!—There was a Branch that, waxing
Wanton o'er the Root he drank from,
At a Draught the Living Water
Drain'd wherewith Himself to crown;
Died the Root—and with it died
The Branch—and barren was brought down!"

---

18 "Kai" which almost signifies "Gigantic King," properly belongs
to KHUSRAU, 3rd King of the Kaianian Dynasty; but is here
borrowed for Parvíz as a more mythical Title than SHAH or KING.
  KHUSRAU PARVÍZ (Chosroc The Victorious), Son of Noshíravan
The Great; slain, after Thirty Years of Prosperous Reign, by his
Son Shirúeh, who, according to some, was in Love with his
Father's Mistress Shírín. See further, Section XXI, for one of the
most dramatic Tragedies in Persian History.

XV

SALÁMÁN heard—the Sea of his Soul was mov'd,
And bubbled up with Jewels, and he said;
"OH SHAH, I am the Slave of thy Desire,
Dust of thy Throne ascending Foot am I;
Whatever thou Desirest I would do,
But sicken of my own Incompetence;
Not in the Hand of my infirmer Will
To carry into Deed mine own Desire.
Time upon Time I torture mine own Soul,
Devising liberation from the Snare
I languish in. But when upon that Moon
I *think*, my Soul relapses—and when *look*—
I leave both Worlds behind to follow her!"

XVI

THE SHAH ceased Counsel, and THE SAGE
   began.
"Oh Thou new Vintage of a Garden old,
Last Blazon of the Pen of 'LET THERE BE,'[19]
Who read'st the SEVEN and FOUR;[20]
   interpretest

---

19 The Pen of "KÛN"—"ESTO!"—The famous Passage of Creation
   stolen from Genesis by the Kurán.
20 Planets?—adding Sun, Moon, and the Nodal Dragon's Head and
   Tail; according to the Sanscrit Astronomy adopted by Persia.

The writing on the Leaves of Night and Day—
Archetype of the Assembly of the World,

I have proposed "The Planets" for those mysterious "SEVEN and FOUR." But there is a large Choice, especially for the ever mystical "SEVEN"—Seven Commandments; 7 Climates; 7 Heavens, etc. The "FOUR" may be the 4 Elements, or even the 4 acknowledged Mahommedan Gospels—namely, The Pentateuch, Psalms, New Testament, and Kurán. For SALÁMÁN, though fabled 'not' of The Faith, yet allegorically represents The Mirror of all Faith, and as The original Form of the Human Soul might be intuitively enlightened with all the Revelations that were to be—might even be, in esoteric Sufíism, The Come and Coming Twelfth Imám who had 'read' all the previous Eleven; it being one Doctrine in the East that it is ever the 'Last' and most perfect Prophet who was 'First' Created and reserved in the Interior Heaven nearest to God till the Time of his Mission should come.

Sir John Chardin quotes Seven Magnificats written in gold upon azure over Shah Abbas' Tomb in the great Mosque at Kóm—composed, he says, "par le docte Hasan-Cazy," mainly in glory of Ali the Darling Imám of Persia, but of which the First Hymn "est tout de Mahomet." This has some passages so very parallel with the Sage's Address to SALÁMÁN, that (knowing how little worth such parallels are, especially in a Country where Magnificent Titles of Honour are stereotyped ready to be lavished on Prophet or Khan) nevertheless really seemed borrowed by "le docte Hasan-Cazy," who probably was hard set to invent any new. They show at least how Jámi saluted his 'Alien' Prince with Titles due to Mahomet's Self, and may perhaps light any curious Reader to a better understanding of these Seven and Four. He calls Mahomet "Infaillible Expositeur des Quatre Livres"—those Gospels;—[So Sir John: but the Kurán being one, this looks rather addrest to Ali than Mahomet.] "Conducteur des huit mobiles" the 8 Heavens of the Planets, says the Editor; "Gouverneur des Sept Parties" the Climates; "Archetype des Choses créées; Instrument de la Création du Monde: le plus relevé de la race d'Adam. Ce Peintre incompréhensible, qui a tiré tout d'un seul Coup de Pinceau 'Koun Fikoun,' n'a jamais fait un si beau portrait que le Globe de ton Visage."

Who hold'st the Key of Adam's Treasury—
(Know thine own Dignity and slight it not,
For Thou art Greater yet than all I tell)—
The Mighty Hand that mix'd thy Dust inscribed
The Character of Wisdom on thy Heart;
Oh Cleanse thy Bosom of Material Form,
And turn the Mirror of the Soul to Spirit,
Until it be with Spirit all possest,
Drown'd in the Light of Intellectual Truth.
Oh veil thine Eyes from Mortal Paramour,
And follow not her Step!—For what is She?—
What is She but a Vice and a Reproach,
Her very Garment-hem Pollution!
For such Pollution madden not thine Eyes,
Waste not thy Body's Strength, nor taint thy Soul,
Nor set the Body and the Soul in Strife!
Supreme is thine Original Degree,
Thy Star upon the Top of Heaven; but Lust
Will fling it down even unto the Dust!"

Quoth a Muezzin unto Crested
Chanticleer—"Oh Voice of Morning,
Not a Sage of all the Sages
Prophesies of Dawn, or startles
At the wing of Time, like Thee.

One so wise methinks were fitter
Perching on the Beams of Heaven,
Than with these poor Hens about him,
Raking in a Heap of Dung."
"And," replied the Cock, "in Heaven
Once I was; but by my Evil
Lust am fallen down to raking
With my wretched Hens about me
On the Dunghill. Otherwise
I were even now in Eden
With the Bird of Paradise."

XVII

When from THE SAGE these words SALÁMÁN
   heard,
The breath of Wisdom round his Palate blew;
He said—"Oh Darling of the Soul of Plato,
To whom a hundred Aristotles bow;
Oh Thou that an Eleventh to the Ten
Original INTELLIGENCES addest,[21]—
I lay my Face before Thee in the Dust,
The humblest Scholar of thy Court am I;
Whose every word I find a Well of Wisdom,
And hasten to imbibe it in my Soul.
But clear unto thy clearest Eye it is,

---

[21] this passage finds its explanation in the last Section.

That Choice is not within Oneself—To Do,
Not in The Will, but in The Power, to Do.
From that which I originally am
How shall I swerve? or how put forth a Sign
Beyond the Power that is by Nature Mine?"

XVIII

Unto the Soul that is confused by Love
Comes Sorrow after Sorrow—most of all
To Love whose only Friendship is Reproof,
And overmuch of Counsel—whereby Love
Grows stubborn, and increases the Disease.
Love unreproved is a delicious food;
Reproved, is Feeding on one's own Heart's
    Blood.
Salámán heard; his Soul came to his Lips;
Reproaches struck not Absál out of him,
But drove Confusion in; bitter became
The Drinking of the sweet Draught of Delight,
And waned the Splendour of his Moon of
    Beauty.
His Breath was Indignation, and his Heart
Bled from the Arrow, and his Anguish grew
—How bear it?—Able to endure one wound,
From Wound on Wound no remedy but Flight;
Day after Day, Design upon Design,

He turn'd the Matter over in his Heart,
And, after all, no Remedy but Flight.
Resolv'd on that, he victuall'd and equipp'd
A Camel, and one Night he led it forth,
And mounted—he and Absál at his side,
The fair SALÁMÁN and ABSÁL the Fair,
Together on one Camel side by side,
Twin Kernels in a single Almond packt.
And True Love murmurs not, however small
His Chamber—nay, the straitest best of all.

When the Moon of Canaan YÚSUF
Darken'd in the Prison of Ægypt,
Night by Night ZULAIKHA went
To see him—for her Heart was broken.
Then to her said One who never
Yet had tasted of Love's Garden:
"Leavest thou thy Palace-Chamber
For the Felon's narrow Cell?"
Answer'd She, "Without my Lover,
Were my Chamber Heaven's Horizon,
It were closer than an Ant's eye;
And the Ant's eye wider were
Than Heaven, my Lover with me there!"

XIX

Six days SALÁMÁN on the Camel rode,
And then Remembrance of foregone Reproach
Abode not by him; and upon the Seventh
He halted on the Seashore, and beheld
An Ocean boundless as the Heaven above,
That, reaching its Circumference from Káf
To Káf, down to the Back of GAU and MANI[22]
Descended, and its Stars were Creatures' Eyes.
The Face of it was as it were a Range
Of moving Mountains; or as endless Hosts
Of Camels trooping from all Quarters up,
Furious, with the Foam upon their Lips.
In it innumerable glittering Fish
Like Jewels polish-sharp, to the sharp Eye
But for an Instant visible, glancing through
As Silver Scissors slice a blue Brocade;
Though were the Dragon from its Hollow
    roused,
The DRAGON of the Stars[23] would stare Aghast.

---

22 The Bull and Fish—the lowest Substantial Base of Earth. "He first
made the Mountains; then cleared the Face of Earth from Sea;
then fixed it fast on Gau; Gau on Mahi; and Mahi on Air; and Air
on what? on NOTHING; Nothing upon Nothing, all is Nothing—
Enough." Attar quoted in De Sacy's Pendnamah, XXXV.

23 The Sidereal Dragon, whose Head, according to the Pauránic (or
Poetic) Astronomers of the East, devoured the Sun and Moon in
Eclipse. "But *we* know," said Ramachandra to Sir W. Jones, "that
the supposed Head and Tail of the Dragon mean only the Nodes,

SALÁMÁN eyed the Sea, and cast about
To cross it—and forthwith upon the Shore
Devis'd a Shallop like a Crescent Moon,
Wherein that Sun and Moon in happy Hour
Enter'd as into some Celestial Sign;
That, figured like a Bow, but Arrow-like
In Flight, was feather'd with a little Sail,
And, pitcht upon the Water like a Duck,
So with her Bosom sped to her Desire.
When they had sail'd their Vessel for a
    Moon,
And marr'd their Beauty with the wind o' th'
    Sea,
Suddenly in mid Sea reveal'd itself
An Isle, beyond Description beautiful;
An Isle that all was Garden; not a Bird
Of Note or Plume in all the World but
    there;
There as in Bridal Retinue array'd
The Pheasant in his Crown, the Dove in her
    Collar;
And those who tuned their Bills among the
    Trees
That Arm in Arm from Fingers paralyz'd
With any Breath of Air Fruit moist and dry

____

or Points formed by Intersections of the Ecliptic and the Moon's
Orbit." Sir W. Jones' Works, Vol. IV. P. 74.

Down scatter'd in Profusion to their Feet,
Where Fountains of Sweet Water ran, and
    round
Sunshine and Shadow chequer-chased the
    Ground.
Here Iram Garden seem'd in Secresy
Blowing the Rosebud of its Revelation;
Or Paradise, forgetful of the Day
Of Audit, lifted from her Face the Veil.
SALÁMÁN saw the Isle, and thought no more
Or Further—there with ABSÁL, he sat down,
ABSÁL and He together side by side
Rejoicing like the Lily and the Rose,
Together like the Body and the Soul.
Under its Trees in one another's Arms
They slept—they drank its Fountains hand in
    hand—
Sought Sugar with the Parrot—or in Sport
Paraded with the Peacock—raced the
    Partridge
Or fell a-talking with the Nightingale.
There was the Rose without a Thorn, and
    there
The Treasure and no Serpent to beware—
What sweeter than your Mistress at your side
In such a Solitude, and none to Chide!

Whisper'd one to WÁMIK[24]—"*Oh Thou*
Victim of the Wound of AZRA,
What is it that like a Shadow
Movest thou about in Silence
Meditating Night and Day?"
WÁMIK *answer'd, "Even this—*
To fly with AZRA *to the Desert;*
There by so remote a Fountain
That, whichever way one travell'd
League on League, one yet should never,
Never meet the Face of Man—
There to pitch my Tent—for ever
There to gaze on my Belovéd;
Gaze, till Gazing out of Gazing
Grew to BEING *Her I gaze on,*
SHE *and I no more, but in One*
Undivided Being blended.
All that is not ONE *must ever*
Suffer with the Wound of Absence;
And whoever in Love's City
Enters, finds but Room for ONE,
And but in ONENESS *Union."*

---

24 Another Typical Lover of Azra, a Virgin.

XX

When by and bye THE SHAH was made
  aware
Of that Soul-wasting absence of his Son,
He reach'd a Cry to Heav'n—his Eyelashes
Wept Blood—Search everywhere he set a-foot,
But none could tell the hidden Mystery.
Then bade he bring a Mirror that he had,
A Mirror, like the Bosom of the Wise,
Reflecting all the World,[25] and lifting up
The Veil from all its Secret, Good and Evil.
That Mirror bade he bring, and, in its Face
Looking, beheld the Face of his Desire.
He saw those Lovers in the Solitude,
Turn'd from the World, and all its ways, and
  People,
And looking only in each other's Eyes,

---

25 Mythically attributed to the East—and in some wild Western
Avatar—to this Shah's Predecessor, Alexander the Great. Perhaps
(V. Hammer thinks) the Concave Mirror upon the Alexandrian
Pharos, which by Night projected such a fiery Eye over the Deep
as not only was fabled to exchange Glances with that on the
Rhodian Colossus, and in Oriental Imagination and Language
to penetrate "THE WORLD," but by Day to Reflect it to him who
looked therein with Eyes to see. The Cup of their own JAMSHÍD
had, whether Full or Empty, the same Property. And that Silver
Cup found in Benjamin's Sack—"Is not this it in which my Lord
drinketh, and whereby indeed he *Divineth*?—Gen. XLIV. 5. Our
Reflecting Telescope is going some way to realize the Alexandrian
Fable.

And never finding any Sorrow there.
THE SHAH beheld them as they were, and
    Pity
Fell on his Eyes, and he reproach'd them not;
And, gathering all their Life into his hand,
Not a Thread lost, disposed in Order all.
Oh for the Noble Nature, and Clear Heart,
That, seeing Two who draw one Breath,
    together
Drinking the Cup of Happiness and Tears
Unshatter'd by the Stone of Separation,
Is loath their sweet Communion to destroy,
Or cast a Tangle in the Skein of Joy.
The Arrows that assail the Lords of SORROW
Come from the Hand of Retribution.
Do Well, that in thy Turn Well may betide
    Thee;
And turn from Ill, that Ill may turn beside Thee.

FIRHÁD, Moulder of the Mountain,
Love-distracted look'd to SHÍRÍN,
And SHÍRÍN the Sculptor's Passion
Saw, and turn'd her Heart to Him.

Then the Fire of Jealous Frenzy
Caught and carried up the Harvest
Of the Might of KAI KHUSRAU.

Plotting with that ancient Hag
Of Fate, the Sculptor's Cup he poison'd,
And remained the Lord of Love.

So—But Fate that Fate avenges
Arms SHIRÚEH with the Dagger,
That at once from SHÍRÍN tore him,
Hurl'd him from the Throne of Glory.[26]

XXI

But as the days went on, and still THE SHAH
Beheld SALÁMÁN now sunk in ABSÁL,
And yet no Hand of better Effort lifted;
But still the Crown that shall adorn his Head,
And still the Throne that waited for his Foot,
Trampled from Memory by a Base Desire,
Of which the Soul was still unsatisfied—
Then from the Sorrow of THE SHAH fell Fire;
To Gracelessness Ungracious he became,
And, quite to shatter his rebellious Lust,

---

26 One Story is that Khusrau had promised if Firhád cut through a
Mountain, and brought a Stream through, Shírín should be his.
Firhád was on the point of achieving his Work, when Khusrau
sent an old Woman (here, perhaps, purposely confounded with
Fate) to tell him Shírín was dead; whereon Firhád threw himself
headlong from the Rock. The Sculpture at Beysitún (or Besitún),
where Rawlinson has decyphered Darius and Xerxes, was
traditionally called Firhád's.

Upon SALÁMÁN all his WILL discharged[27].
And Lo! SALÁMÁN to his Mistress turn'd,
But could not reach her—look'd and look'd
   again,
And palpitated tow'rd her—but in Vain!
Oh Misery! what to the Bankrupt worse
Than Gold he cannot reach! To one athirst
Than Fountain to the Eye and Lip forbid!—
Or than Heaven opened to the Eyes in Hell!—
Yet, when SALÁMÁN's Anguish was extreme,
The Door of Mercy open'd in his Face;
He saw and knew his Father's Hand
   outstretcht
To lift him from Perdition—timidly,
Timidly tow'rd his Father's Face his own
He lifted, Pardon-pleading, Crime-contest,
As the stray Bird one day will find her Nest.

A Disciple ask'd a Master,
"By what Token should a Father
Vouch for his reputed Son?"
Said the Master, "By the Stripling,
Howsoever Late or Early,
Like to the reputed Father
Growing—whether Wise or Foolish."

---

27 He Mesmerizes Him!—See also further on this Power of the Will
  in Sections XXIII. and XXVI.

"Lo the disregarded Darnel
With itself adorns the Wheat-field,
And for all the Early Season
Satisfies the Farmer's Eye;
But come once the Hour of Harvest,
And another Grain shall answer,
'Darnel and no Wheat, am I'."

XXII

When THE SHAH saw SALÁMÁN's face again,
And breath'd the Breath of Reconciliation,
He laid the Hand of Love upon his Shoulder,
The Kiss of Welcome on his Cheek, and said,
"Oh Thou, who lost, Love's Banquet lost its
    Salt,
And Mankind's Eye its Pupil!—Thy Return
Is as another Sun to Heaven; a new
Rose blooming in the Garden of the Soul.
Arise, Oh Moon of Majesty unwaned!
The Court of the Horizon is thy Court,
Thy Kingdom is the Kingdom of the World!—
Lo! Throne and Crown await Thee—Throne
    and Crown
Without thy Impress but uncurrent Gold,
Not to be stamp'd by one not worthy Them;
Behold! The Rebel's Face is at thy Door;

Let him not triumph—let the Wicked dread
The Throne under thy Feet, the Crown upon
    thy Head.
Oh Spurn them not behind Thee! Oh my Son,
Wipe Thou the Woman's Henna from thy
    Hand:
Withdraw Thee from the Minion who from
    Thee
Dominion draws;[28] the Time is come to choose,
Thy Mistress or the World to hold or lose."
Four are the Signs of Kingly Aptitude;
Wise Head—clean Heart—strong Arm —and
    open Hand.
Wise is He not—Continent cannot be—
Who binds himself to an unworthy Lust;
Nor Valiant, who submits to a weak Woman;
Nor Liberal, who cannot draw his Hand
From that in which so basely he is busied.
And of these Four who misses All or One
Is not the Bridegroom of Dominion.

XXIII

Ah the poor Lover!—In the changing Hands
Of Day and Night no wretcheder than He!

---

28 "*Shah*" and "*Sháhid*" (Mistress)—a sort of Punning the Persian
    Poets are fond of.

No Arrow from the Bow of Evil Fate
But reaches him—one Dagger at his Throat,
Another comes to wound him from behind.
Wounded by Love—then wounded by Reproof
Of Loving—and, scarce stauncht the Blood of
    Shame
By flying from his Love—then, worst of all,
Love's back-blow of Revenge for having fled!
SALÁMÁN heard—he rent the Robe of Peace
He came to loathe his Life, and long for
    Death,
(For better Death itself than Life in Death)
He turn'd his face with ABSÁL to the Desert—
Enter'd the deadly Plain; Branch upon Branch
Cut down, and gather'd in a lofty Pile,
And fired. They look'd upon the Flames, those
    Two
They look'd, and they rejoiced; and hand in
    hand
They sprang into the Fire. THE SHAH who
    saw,
In secret all had order'd; and the Flame,
Directed by his Self-fulfilling WILL,
Devouring utterly ABSÁL, pass'd by
SALÁMÁN harmless—the pure Gold return'd
Entire, but all the baser Metal burn'd.

XXIV

Heaven's Dome is but a wondrous House of
    Sorrow,
And Happiness therein a lying Fable.
When first they mix'd the Clay of Man, and
    cloth'd
His Spirit in the Robe of Perfect Beauty,
For Forty Mornings did an Evil Cloud
Rain Sorrows over him from Head to Foot;
And when the Forty Mornings pass'd to
    Night,
Then came one Morning-Shower—one
    Morning-Shower
Of Joy—to Forty of the Rain of Sorrow!—
And though the better Fortune came at last
To seal the Work, yet every Wise Man knows
Such Consummation never can be here!
SALÁMÁN fired the Pile; and in the Flame
That, passing him, consumed ABSÁL like
    Straw,
Died his Divided Self, and there survived
His Individual; and, like a Body
From which the Soul is parted, all alone.
Then rose his Cry to Heaven—his Eyelashes
Dropt Blood—his Sighs stood like a Smoke in
    Heaven,

And Morning rent her Garment at his
    Anguish.[29]
He tore his Bosom with his Nails—he smote
Stone on his Bosom—looking then on hands
No longer lockt in hers, and lost their Jewel,
He tore them with his Teeth. And when came
    Night,
He hid him in some Corner of the House,
And communed with the Fantom of his Love.
"Oh Thou whose Presence so long sooth'd my
    Soul,
Now burnt with thy Remembrance! Oh so
    long
The Light that fed these Eyes now dark with
    Tears!
Oh Long, Long Home of Love now lost for
    Ever!
We were Together—that was all Enough—
We two rejoicing in each other's Eyes,
Infinitely rejoicing—all the World
Nothing to Us, nor We to all the World—
No Road to reach us, nor an Eye to watch—
All Day we whisper'd in each other's Ears,
All Night we slept in one another's Arms—
All seem'd to our Desire, as if the Hand

---

29 "When the Cloud of Spring beheld the Evil Disposition of Time,
    Its Weeping fell upon the Jessamine and Hyacinth and Wild
    Rose."—*Háfiz.*

Of unjust Fortune were for once too short.
Oh would to God that when I lit the Pyre
The Flame had left Thee Living and me Dead,
Not Living worse than Dead, depriv'd of Thee!
Oh were I but with Thee!—at any Cost
Stript of this terrible Self-solitude!
Oh but with Thee Annihilation—lost,
Or in Eternal Intercourse renew'd!"

Slumber-drunk an Arab in the
Desert off his Camel tumbled,
Who the lighter of her Burden
Ran upon her road rejoicing.
When the Arab woke at morning,
Rubb'd his Eyes and look'd about him—
"Oh my Camel! Oh my Camel!"
Quoth he, "Camel of my Soul!—
That Lost with Her I lost might be,
Or found, She might be found with Me!"

XXV

When in this Plight THE SHAH Salámán saw,
His Soul was struck with Anguish, and the Vein
Of Life within was strangled—what to do
He knew not. Then he turn'd him to THE
    SAGE—

"Oh Altar of the World, to whom Mankind
Directs the Face of Prayer in Weal or Woe,
Nothing but Wisdom can untie the Knot;
And art not Thou the Wisdom of the World,
The Master-Key of all its Difficulties?
ABSÁL is perisht; and, because of Her,
SALÁMÁN dedicates his Life to Sorrow;
I cannot bring back Her, nor comfort Him.
Lo, I have said! My Sorrow is before Thee;
From thy far-reaching Wisdom help Thou Me
Fast in the Hand of Sorrow! Help Thou Me,
For I am very wretched!" Then THE SAGE—
"Oh Thou that err'st not from the Road of
        Right,
If but SALÁMÁN have not broke my Bond,
Nor lies beyond the Noose of my Firmán,
He quickly shall unload his Heart to me,
And I will find a Remedy for all."

XXVI

Then THE SAGE counsell'd, and SALÁMÁN
        heard,
And drew the Wisdom down into his Heart;
And, sitting in the Shadow of the Perfect,
His Soul found Quiet under; sweet it seem'd,
Sweeping the Chaff and Litter from his own,

To be the very Dust of Wisdom's Door,
Slave of the Firmán of the Lord of Life.
Then THE SAGE marvell'd at his Towardness,
And wrought in Miracle in his behalf.
He pour'd the Wine of Wisdom in his Cup,
He laid the Dew of Peace upon his lips;
And when Old Love return'd to Memory,
And broke in Passion from his Lips, THE
    SAGE,
Under whose waxing WILL Existence rose
Responsive, and, relaxing, waned again,
Raising a Fantom Image of ABSÁL,
Set it awhile before SALÁMÁN's Eyes,
Till, having sow'd the Seed of Quiet there,
It went again down to Annihilation.
But ever, for the Sum of his Discourse,
THE SAGE would tell of a Celestial Love;
"ZUHRAH,"[30] he said, "the Lustre of the Stars
'Fore whom the Beauty of the Brightest wanes;
Who were she to reveal her perfect Beauty,
The Sun and Moon would craze; ZUHRAH," he
    said,
"The Sweetness of the Banquet—none in Song
Like Her—her Harp filling the Ear of Heaven,
That Dervish-dances at her Harmony."
SALÁMÁN listen'd, and inclin'd—again

---

30 The Planetary and Celestial Venus.

Repeated, Inclination ever grew;
Until THE SAGE beholding in his Soul
The Spirit[31] quicken, so effectually
With ZUHRAH wrought, that she reveal'd
   herself
In her pure Beauty to SALÁMÁN's Soul,
And washing ABSÁL's Image from his Breast,
There reign'd instead. Celestial Beauty seen,
He left the Earthly; and, once come to know
Eternal Love, he let the Mortal go.

XXVII

The Crown of Empire how supreme a Lot!
The Throne of the Sultan how high!—But not
For All—None but the Heaven-ward Foot may
   dare
To mount—The Head that touches Heaven to
   wear!
When the Belov'd of Royal Augury
Was rescued from the Bondage of ABSÁL,
Then he arose, and shaking off the Dust
Of that lost Travel, girded up his Heart,
And look'd with undefiléd Robe to Heaven.
Then was His Head worthy to wear the Crown,

---

31 "Maany." The Mystical pass-word of the Súfís, to express the
  Transcendental New Birth of The Soul.

His Foot to mount the Throne. And then THE
   SHAH
Summon'd the Chiefs of Cities and of States,
Summon'd the Absolute Ones who wore the
   Ring,
And such a Banquet order'd as is not
For Sovereign Assemblement the like
In the Folding of the Records of the World.
No arméd Host, nor Captain of a Host,
From all the Quarters of the World, but there;
Of whom not one but to SALÁMÁN did
Obeisance, and lifted up his Neck
To yoke it under his Supremacy.
Then THE SHAH crown'd him with the
   Golden Crown,
And set the Golden Throne beneath his Feet,
And over all the Heads of the Assembly,
And in the Ears of all of them, his Jewels
With the Diamond of Wisdom cut and said:—

XXVIII

"My Son,[32] the Kingdom of The World is not
Eternal, nor the Sum of right Desire;

---

32 One sees Jámí taking Advantage of his Allegorical Shah to read a
   Lesson to the Real—whose Ears Advice, unlike Praise, scarce ever
   reached unless obliquely. The Warning (and doubtless with good
   Reason) is principally aimed at the Minister.

Make thou the Faith-preserving Intellect
Thy Counsellor; and considering To-day
To-MORROW's Seed-field, ere That come to
    bear,
Sow with the Harvest of Eternity.
All Work with Wisdom hath to do—by that
Stampt current only; what Thyself to do
Art wise, that DO; what not, consult the Wise.
Turn not thy Face away from the old Ways,
That were the Canon of the Kings of Old;
Nor cloud with Tyranny the Glass of Justice;
But rather strive that all Confusion
Change by thy Justice to its opposite.
In whatsoever Thou shalt Take or Give
Look to the HOW; Giving and Taking still,
Not by the backward Counsel of the Godless,
But by the Law of FAITH increase and Give.
Drain not thy People's purse—the Tyranny
Which Thee enriches at thy Subjects' cost,
Awhile shall make Thee strong; but in the End
Shall bow thy Neck beneath a Double Burden.
The Tyrant goes to Hell—follow not Him—
Become not Thou the Fuel of its Fires.
Thou art a Shepherd, and thy Flock the
    People,
To save and not destroy; nor at their Loss
To lift Thyself above the Shepherd's calling.

For which is for the other, Flock or Shepherd?
And join with Thee true Men to keep the Flock.
Dogs, if you will—but Trusty—head in leash,
Whose Teeth are for the Wolf, not for the Lamb,
And least of all the Wolf's Accomplices,
Their Jaws blood-dripping from the Tyrant's
    Shambles.
For Shahs must have Vizírs—but be they Wise
And Trusty—knowing well the Realm's Estate-
(For who eats Profit of a Fool? and least
A wise King girdled by a Foolish Council—)
Knowing how far to Shah and Subject bound
On either Hand—not by Extortion,
Nor Usury wrung from the People's purse,
Their Master's and their own Estates (to whom
Enough is apt enough to make them Rebel)
Feeding to such a Surplus as feeds Hell.
Proper in Soul and Body be They—pitiful
To Poverty—hospitable to the Saint—
Their sweet Access a Salve to wounded Hearts,
Their Vengeance terrible to the Evil Doer,
Thy Heralds through the Country bringing
    Thee
Report of Good or Ill—which to confirm
By thy peculiar Eye—and least of all
Suffering Accuser also to be Judge—
By surest Steps builds up Prosperity."

Epilogue

XXIX

Under the Outward Form of any Story
An Inner Meaning lies—This Story now
Completed, do Thou of its Mystery
(Whereto the Wise hath found himself a way)
Have thy Desire—No Tale of *I* and *THOU*,
Though *I* and *THOU* be its Interpreters.[33]
What signifies THE SHAH? and what THE
    SAGE?
And what SALÁMÁN not of Woman born?
And what ABSÁL who drew him to Desire?
And what THE KINGDOM that awaited him
When he had drawn his Garment from her
    Hand?
What means THE FIERY PILE? and what
    THE SEA?
And what that Heavenly ZUHRAH who at
    last
Clear'd ABSÁL from the Mirror of his Soul?

---

33 The Story is of 'Generals,' though enacted by 'Particulars.'

291

Learn part by part the Mystery from me;
All Ear from Head to Foot and Understanding
   be.

XXX

The Incomparable Creator, when this World
He did create, created First of All
THE FIRST INTELLIGENCE[34]—First of a Chain
Of Ten Intelligences, of which the Last
Sole Agent is in this our Universe,
ACTIVE INTELLIGENCE so call'd; The One
Distributor of Evil and of Good,

---

34 "These Intelligences are only another Form of the Neo-Platonic
Dæmones. The Neo-Platonists held that Matter and Spirit could
have no Intercourse—they were, as it were, '*incommensurate.*'
How then, granting this premise, was Creation possible? Their
answer was a kind of gradual Elimination. God the "Ætus Purus,"
created an Œon; this Œon created a Second; and so on, until
the Tenth Œon was sufficiently Material (as the Ten were in a
continually descending Series) to affect Matter, and so cause the
Creation by giving to Matter the Spiritual 'Form.'

Similarly we have in Súfíism these Ten Intelligences in a
corresponding Series, and for the same End.

There are Ten Intelligences, and Nine Heavenly Spheres, of
which the Ninth is the Uppermost Heaven, appropriated to the
First Intelligence; the Eighth, that of the Zodiac, to the Second;
the Seventh, Saturn, to the Third; the Sixth, Jupiter, to the Fourth;
the Fifth, Mars, to the Fifth; the Fourth, The Sun, to the Sixth; the
Third, Venus, to the Seventh; the Second, Mercury, to the Eighth;
the First, The Moon, to the Ninth; and THE EARTH is the peculiar
Sphere of the TENTH, or lowest Intelligence, called THE ACTIVE."

Of Joy and Sorrow, Himself apart from
     MATTER,
In Essence and in Energy—his Treasure
Subject to no such Talisman—He yet
Hath fashion'd all that is—Material Form,
And Spiritual, sprung from HIM—by HIM
Directed all, and in his Bounty drown'd.
Therefore is He that Firmán-issuing SHAH
To whom the World was subject. But because
What He distributes to the Universe
Himself from still a Higher Power receives,
The Wise, and all who comprehend aright,
Will recognise that Higher in THE SAGE.
His the PRIME SPIRIT that, spontaneously
Projected by the TENTH INTELLIGENCE,
Was from no Womb of MATTER reproduced
A Special Essence called THE SOUL—A CHILD
Fresh sprung from Heaven in Raiment
     undefiled
Of Sensual Taint, and therefore call'd
     SALÁMÁN.
And who ABSÁL—The Lust-adoring Body,
Slave to the Blood and Sense—through whom
     THE SOUL,
Although the Body's very Life it be,
Does yet imbibe the Knowledge and Desire
Of Things of SENSE; and these united thus

By such a Tie God only can unloose,
BODY AND SOUL are Lovers Each of other.
What is THE SEA on which He sail'd?—The
  Sea
Of Animal Desire—the Sensual Abyss,
Under whose Waters lie a World of Being
Swept far from God in that Submersion.
And wherefore was it ABSÁL in that Isle
Deceived in her Delight, and that SALÁMÁN
Fell short of his Desire?—That was to show
How Passion tires, and how with Time begins
The Folding of the Carpet of DESIRE
And what the turning of SALÁMÁN's Heart
Back to THE SHAH, and looking to the
  Throne
Of Pomp and Glory? What but the Return
Of the LOST SOUL to its true Parentage,
And back from Carnal Error looking up
Repentant to its Intellectual Throne.
What is THE FIRE?—Ascetic Discipline,
That burns away the Animal Alloy,
Till all the Dross of MATTER be consumed,
And the Essential Soul, its raiment clean
Of Mortal Taint, be left. But forasmuch
As any Life-long Habit so consumed,
May well recur a Pang for what is lost,
Therefore THE SAGE set in SALÁMÁN's Eyes

A Soothing Fantom of the Past, but still
Told of a Better Venus, till his Soul
She fill'd, and blotted out his Mortal Love.
For what is ZUHRAH?—That Divine
    Perfection,
Wherwith the Soul inspir'd and all array'd
In Intellectual Light is Royal blest,
And mounts THE THRONE, and wears THE
    CROWN, and Reigns
Lord of the Empire of Humanity.
This is the Meaning of This Mystery
Which to know wholly ponder in thy Heart,
Till all its ancient Secret be enlarged.
Enough—The written Summary I close,
And set my Seal:

            THE TRUTH GOD ONLY KNOWS.

APPENDIX

What follows concerning the Royal Game of Chúgán comes from the Appendix to Vol. 1. of Sir William Ouseley's Travels in the East.

Firdúsi tells of Siavesh and his Iranian (Persian) Heroes astonishing AFRASIÁB of TURÁN with their Skill at this Game 600 years before Christ; and GUSHTASP (Hystaspes), to the sound of Drum and Trumpet, drives the Ball Invisible with his Blow. Nizámi sets Shírín and her Maidens playing at it, against her King, Khusrau Parvíz, and his Ministers;

> "On one side was the Moon and her Stars,
>   On the other THE SHAH and his Firmán-
>   bearers."

Ouseley however (allowing for Poetic License) believes the Game was played "through almost every Reign of the Sassanian Dynasty—as much esteemed by the Mahommedan Kings as by their Fire-worshipping Predecessors."

"We find the Greek Emperor, Manuel Commenus, with his Byzantine Princes and Nobles, enjoying this Amusement on Horse-back in the 12th Century; the Wooden Ball having been exchanged for one more soft, form'd of stuff'd Leather; and the Stick, or Wand, instead of a Hammer-like Head, terminating in a Hoop; which, as our Battledores or Tennis-rackets, presented to the Ball a reticulated space. This Imperial Sport is well described by the Historian Cinnamus, who probably was a Spectator." It went by the slightly altered name Tsukanisterion—which word, however, since Chúgán means the Bandy-stick employed, more properly signifies, I suppose, the Ground played on; and equally related to the Persian, had they chosen to affix, as so often, the Verb common to themselves, the Greeks, the Latins, and us, and called the place of Exercise Chúgán *istán*; or Chúgán-stand.

Piétro della Valle, who saw it played in SHAH ABBAS' time (1618), calls it "Pallamaglio," and found both Game and Name subsisting in the Florentine "Calcio"—only that the Florentine played a-foot, and the Persian "piu nobilmente à Cavallo." The Spanish Jesuit Ovalle found it also (also on Foot) under the name of "Chueca," in South America, in 1646.

Ducange finds Name and Game also in the "Chicane" of Languedoc, from which he naturally thinks it borrowed; not daring to push Derivation to the English word "Chiquen," he says, "qui signifie un Poullet; en sorte que 'Chiquaner' seroit imiter les Poullets qui ont coutûme de courir les uns apres les autres pour arracher les morceaux du Bec," etc.

Englishmen know the Game well (on Foot too, and with such Leather Balls as the Persians perhaps knew not how to harden), under many Forms and Names—Golf, Stow-Ball, Shinty, Hocky, Bandy, etc.

Though the Sticks, or Bats, are here represented long, they really were (as Chardin and others report) so short as to cause the Rider to stoop below the Saddlebow to strike; which, the Horse going full gallop, was great part of the Difficulty. And Tabri describes Events in the Eighth Century (just before his own Time), when Harun Alraschid was still little, so that when on Horseback, "he could not reach to strike the Ball with a Chúgán." Ouseley thinks the Chúgán sticks were only *generally*, or partially. semicircular at the striking End. But that they were so (varying perhaps a little in degree as our Bandy sticks do) is proved by the Text of the Present Poem, as also by a previous line in the Original, where—

"The Realm of Existence is the space of his
    Meidan,
The Ball of Heaven in the Crook of his Chúgán."

And passages in Hafíz speak of his Heart as being carried off by his Beloved's Eyebrow; which no Persian Lover ever dreamt of but as arched indeed.

As the "Fair One" of Persian Mysticism is the Deity's Self—so the Points of that Beauty (as in our Canticles) adumbrate so many of the Deity's Attributes; varying however with various Poets, or their Commentators. Sir W. Jones speaks of THE HAIR as emblematic of "The Expansion of Divine Glory"—The Lips as of "Hidden Mysteries"—The Down of the Cheek as "Spirits round the Throne," whose central point of excessive Light is darken'd into the Mole upon the Cheek!—Tholuck, from a Turkish Commentary, interprets the Ringlets as "The Divine Mysteries;" the Forehead their Manifestation, etc.

The Beauty of ABSÁL, though Sensual, yet seduces SALÁMÁN (The Soul) with its Likeness to the Divine; and her Tresses, as we see, play their part, involving him in their Intricacies.

GLOSSARY

ALIF [*a'-lif*] The first letter in the Persian alphabet.

ALLAH [*al'-lā*] Arabic name for God. The Absolute.

AMIR [*a-meer'*] Prince.

ASSÁR [*as'-sār*] Oil pressers.

ATTÁR [*at'-tār*] Druggist.

ATTÁR The persian poet Farrîd-uddîn Attâr, author of *The Mantiq al-Tayr*, i.e., Discourse of the Birds.

BAHRÁM GUR [*bah'-rām goor*] Bahram of the Wild Ass, Persian king and hunter.

CARAVANSERAI [*kar-a-van'-se-ray*] Inn where caravans rest at night.

DANAD He knows, third person singular of *dân*, to know.

FENUSI KHIYAL [*fā-noo'-see khee'-yal*] Magic lantern.

FERRÁSH [*fer-rāsh'*] Servant, tent-pitcher.

HÁFIZ [*hā-fiz*] Persian lyric poet (d. 1389).

HÁTIM TAI [*hā-tim tye*] A pre-Islamic Arab famed for his generosity.

HIJRA, more commonly HEGIRA [*he-jye-ra*] The migration of Muhammad from Mecca to Medina in AD 622 from which Muslims date their era.

IMÁM [*i-mām'*] A Muhamadan leader of prayer.

IRAM [*ee'-ram*] A fabulous garden supposed to have been planted in Arabia by Shaddád bin Ad.

JÁMI [*jā-mi*] Persian poet (d. 1492).

JAMSHÝD [*Jam'-sheed*] Mythical Persian king. According to Firdausi he reigned seven hundred years. His palace was at Persepolis.

JELÁLUDDÍN [*je-lāl'-ud-deen*] Malikshah. A Saljuk sultán (1072–1092).

KAIKHOSRÚ [*Kye'-khos-roo*] Mythical Persian king.

KAIKOBÁD [*kye'-ko-bād*] Mythical king.

KHORÁSÁN [*kho-rā-sán'*] The largest of the Persian provinces where Omar was born.

KUZA-NAMA [*koo'-za nā'-ma*] Book of pots, title given to stanzas 59–66 in first edition of the *Rubáiyat*.

MÁH Moon.

MÁHI Fish.

MAHMUD [*mah'-mood*] King of Ghazna, b. 969, d. 1030.

MIHRÁB [*mee-rāb*] The niche in a mosque which indicates the direction of Mecca towards which the Muslim worshipper turns in prayer.

MUEZZIN [*moo-ez'-zin*] Muhammadan crier of the hour of prayer.

MUSHTARI [*mush'-ta-ree*] The planet Jupiter.

NAISHÁPÚR [*nay'-shā-poor*] Nishapur, the city of Khorásán, Iran, where Omar was born'

NOW ROOZ New Year's Day.

NIZÁM UL MULK [*nee-zām' ool moolk'*] Vizier to Alp Arslan the Younger.

OMAR KHAYYÁM [*o'-mar khye-yahm'*] Persian philosopher, astronomer and poet, author of *The Rubáiyát*, who died in 1132.

PARWÍN [*par'-ween*] The constellation of the Pleiades.

PEHLEVÍ [*peh'-le-vee*] The principal language of the Persians from the third to the ninth centuries AD.

RAMAZÁN [*ram-a-zán*] Ramadan, the ninth month of the Muhammadan year, devoted to strict fasting.

RUBÁIYÁT [*roo'-bye-yat*] Plural of the Arabic word *rubáiyáh*, a quatrain or stanza of four lines.

RUSTUM [*rus'-tum*] A mythical Persian hero, son of Zál and father of Sohráb in the *Shah-nama*.

SÁKÍ [*sā-kee*] Cupbearer.

SHAH-NAMA *The Book of Kings* by Abul Kasim Mansur, better known as Firdausî.

SHEIKH [*shaykh*] An Arabian chief; literally, old man.

SUBHI KAZIB [*soob'-hee kā'-zib*] False dawn.

SUBHI SADIK [*soob'-hee sā'-dik*] True dawn.

SÚFI [*soo'-fee*] Muhammadan mystic. The elaborate Súfi symbolism was much used by the poets.

SULTÁN [*sul-tán*] King.

TAKHALLUS [*ta-khal-lus*] Pen-name used by Persian poets; for example, Abul Kasim Mansur, author of the *Shah-nama*, called himself Firdausî from

Firdaus which means *Paradise*. Omar called himself Khayyám, i.e., Tent-maker.

TAMÁM [*ta-mám*] The end.

TAMÁM SHUD [*ta-mám' shood*] The very end.

YIZIER [*vi-zeer'*] A minister or counsellor of state.

ZÁL [*zál*] The father of Rustum.